ANATOMY OF FITNESS 501

Pilates Exercises

Published by Hinkler Books Pty Ltd 2018
45–55 Fairchild Street
Heatherton Victoria 3202 Australia
www.hinkler.com

hinkler

Created by Moseley Road Inc.
Cover Designer: Sam Grimmer
Prepress: Splitting Image
Production Director: Adam Moore
Designer: Tina Vaughan
Photographer: Naila Ruechel
Author: Audra Avizienis

ISBN: 978 1 4889 3410 0

Printed and bound in Canada

GENERAL DISCLAIMER

The contents of this book are intended to provide useful information to the general public. All materials,
including texts, graphics, and images, are for informational purposes only and are not a substitute for
medical diagnosis, advice, or treatment for specific medical conditions. All readers should seek expert
medical care and consult their own physicians before commencing any exercise program or for any
general or specific health issues. The author and publishers do not recommend or endorse specific
treatments, procedures, advice, or other information found in this book and specifically disclaim
all responsibility for any and all liability, loss, or risk, personal or otherwise, which is incurred as a
consequence, directly or indirectly, of the use or application of any of the material in this publication.

ANATOMY OF FITNESS

501

Pilates Exercises

Craft perfect workouts for your own training goals
and discover the amazing hidden structure of your body

Contents

Chapter Two—Machine and Arc Barrel Exercises 118

Introduction

Mind—body health

501 Pilates Exercises will take you on an invigorating journey to a stronger, sleeker body. Anyone, at any age, can practice Pilates and reap the benefits of this unique mind—body exercise system. Pilates is a low-impact form of exercise that strengthens the body and improves flexibility and balance. Pilates incorporates deep breathing with slow, precise movements that engage the body, mind, and spirit. Whether you perform the exercises on a mat in the privacy of your home or on equipment in a studio, you are bound to feel the energizing effects of a Pilates workout.

History

Founder Joseph Pilates was born in 1883 in a small German town near Düsseldorf. As a youth, he suffered from asthma, rickets, and rheumatic fever, and was bullied for his Greek name and small stature. The young Pilates resolved to overcome his physical adversities. Inspired by his naturopath mother and gymnast father, Pilates educated himself about anatomy and practiced yoga, gymnastics, and martial arts. He became fascinated with the ancient Greek ideal of the human body. At the age of 14, Pilates was already so physically fit that he modeled for anatomical illustrations for books.

In 1912, Pilates emigrated to England, where he worked as a professional boxer and circus performer, posing as a Live Greek Statue. He also trained police officers in self-defense in Scotland Yard. During World War I, Pilates was forced into an internment camp for resident aliens. While there, he developed his first series of exercises, now known as Pilates mat work. At a second internment, at the Isle of Man, Pilates served as a nurse—physiotherapist for bedridden patients. Determined to rehabilitate them, he devised ingenious exercise equipment using the few props available to

him: bed frames and mattress springs. The prototype bed-like structures with pulleys and resistance springs remain the basic design of Pilates machines like the reformer. Contrary to popular belief, Pilates believed that bed rest was detrimental to one's health. Indeed, when a vicious strain of influenza afflicted many of the internees, all of Pilates's patients managed to survive. Convinced that the key to health and physical fitness was a balanced mind—body approach to exercise, Pilates integrated that notion into an exercise system that he called "Contrology."

After the war, Pilates returned to Germany and further refined his exercise method, collaborating with dancers and athletes. In 1923, he rebuffed an offer to train the German Army. Instead, Pilates set sail for the United States and met his future wife during the voyage. Joseph and Clara settled in New York and opened a Contrology studio next door to the New York City Ballet. Their fitness program quickly caught on with elite dancers and performers who sought a low-impact workout to improve their strength, balance, and coordination. Among the Pilates clientele were dancers George Balanchine and Martha Graham and actress Katharine Hepburn. Joseph and Clara continued teaching their craft for more than 40 years.

Gradually, Pilates evolved from a niche exercise method for elite performers into a worldwide phenomenon. Now nearly 10 million people practice Pilates in the United States alone.

Method

Modern Pilates instructors have distilled six guiding principles from the original teachings of Joseph Pilates. The following are the fundamental concepts of the Pilates method as it is taught today.

Control

The central premise of Pilates is mindful control of the body. Pilates exercises should flow from beginning to end in a synchronized manner: anchoring the body correctly, aligning the spine, breathing properly, engaging the abdominals, and activating the appropriate muscles. By training your mind to thoughtfully execute each exercise, you are less likely to suffer an injury or cause stress on your joints and muscles. Not surprisingly, physiotherapists often borrow exercises from Pilates to help rehabilitate their patients.

Centering

In Pilates, all movement emanates from the center of the body. The core muscles are the primary source of strength, stability, and energy. By consciously and correctly engaging the "powerhouse" muscles, in the area below the ribcage down to the pelvic floor, all secondary muscles move more smoothly. Centering also requires proper alignment along the spine to help improve posture and balance, and to develop muscles equally on both sides of the body.

Breathing

For centuries, fitness disciplines such as yoga and tai chi have embraced purposeful breathing to enhance relaxation and performance. Joseph Pilates believed that most people breathe inefficiently, taking shallow breaths mainly from the upper portion of their lungs. His method calls for deep lateral breathing, in which the intercostal muscles along the ribs expand outward. Lateral breathing, unlike lower diaphragmatic breathing, allows the abdominal muscles to remain contracted and stable during exercise.

Another benefit of lateral breathing is that it draws oxygen into the lower lobes of the lungs, where it most efficiently circulates into the bloodstream. Lateral breathing also improves mobility of the ribcage, spine, and shoulder blades.

To practice lateral breathing, begin by lying on the floor with knees bent and head supported. Place your hands on your ribcage with middle fingers touching. Inhale deeply through your nose and focus on expanding your ribcage to the sides and the back. Your fingertips should separate while your upper chest, shoulders, and lower abdomen should remain still.

Pilates also has specific breathing patterns. Generally, you inhale to prepare for an exercise and exhale during the muscle contraction. In the classic Hundred exercise, you regulate your breathing to coordinate with the movement of the exercise, exhaling and inhaling for a specific count while pulsing the arms.

Concentration
The mind–body connection is fundamental to Pilates. Visualize the steps as you prepare, and concentrate on breathing properly. Focus on correct body position, and execute each exercise thoughtfully. Your mind should be fully connected to the experience.

Precision
Pilates exercises consist of precise movements performed in a slow and deliberate manner. Activate all the relevant muscles in the correct sequence for the most benefit from each exercise. In Pilates, the quality of performing an exercise is far more important than the quantity of repetitions.

Flow
Flow through the exercises gracefully like a dancer or a gymnast, with smooth, even movements that are synchronized with your breathing. Avoid jerky motions that may result in injury. Move fluidly from one exercise to the next.

Powerhouse muscles
The powerhouse muscles are the seat of the body's energy, stability, and power. Joseph Pilates coined the term, which refers to the muscles circling around the lumbar spine, from the navel to the pelvic floor and around the torso. He believed that developing this pelvic "girdle of strength" improves posture, balance, and breathing.

Home or studio workouts

Working out at home offers the advantages of setting your own schedule and exercising in private. You don't need a lot of space for mat work; a clean quiet corner of your home will do the trick. A mirror is beneficial to see your form as you practice the exercises. At home, you can listen to relaxing music or place inspirational items nearby. Working out at home, though, is not for everyone because it requires self-motivation. You might also be limited only to mat work if space is an issue.

To add variety to your mat work, you can supplement with some Pilates props. A fitness ball is great for developing balance and joint stability. The magic circle, or resistance ring, is a popular Pilates accessory for arm and leg presses. Resistance bands and weights are also versatile exercise props that build strength.

If you're a beginner, consider taking a few classes first and work with professional instructors who can help you perfect your form. Pilates studios offer more structured workouts for both mat work and apparatus classes. Given the hefty size of most Pilates machines, studio classes may be your only viable option if you're interested in apparatus workouts.

The apparatuses may appeal to beginners because of the built-in cues for body placement: Many of the machines have shoulder pads, headrests, and foot bars as guides. The extra resistance from the springs and pulleys also increases the intensity of the workout.

Whichever type of Pilates you prefer, mat work or machines, you will soon notice the difference in your body—longer, sleeker muscles, a well-defined torso, and a calmer state of mind.

Get started

As with any new fitness regimen, please consult with a physician if you have any injuries or health issues.

The 501 exercises within these pages contain the classic Pilates exercises—such as the Hundred, the Roll-Up, and the Corkscrew—along with dozens of variations that have evolved over the years. Joseph Pilates once said, "Physical fitness is the first requisite of happiness," so get started and enjoy your workouts!

Pilates catchphrases

Articulating the spine/peeling the spine: Moving one vertebra at a time to activate the spine and improve flexibility. Similar terms include "curling up" and "rolling down."

C-curve: The back is flexed, forming a curved C-shape from head to tailbone. The abs are scooped in.

Navel to spine: A classic cue from Joseph Pilates to pull the abdominal muscles up and in toward the spine. Best performed on an exhale to stabilize the torso.

Neutral position: A slight curve in the lower back to avoid straining the back.

Oppositional energy/two-way energy: Exerting energy in opposite directions; for example, lengthening the spine by simultaneously pulling from the top of the head and pressing down with the feet, or extending the arms out to the sides, reaching away from the body, and releasing energy through the fingertips.

Pilates stance: A foot position with heels together and toes turned out at 45 degrees to form a V-shape. The rotation originates in the hips and engages the deep psoas muscles, the only muscles that connect the spine and the legs. Also known as V-stance or V-feet.

Parallel stance: A leg position with hip joints directly above the knees and ankles. The feet are about 6 inches (15 cm) apart.

Popping the ribs: Splaying open the ribs tends to destabilize the torso and overarch the back.

Scooping in the abs: Pulling the deep abdominal muscles up and in to stabilize the body and support the back. Assist the movement by lifting the ribcage and lengthening the spine.

Slide the shoulders down the back: Relaxing the shoulders by pulling the shoulder blades, or scapulae, down the back. This movement also opens the chest.

Stacking: Aligning parts of the body, as in lining up the vertebrae to "stack the spine," or lining up the hips directly above the knees and ankles.

Tabletop position: A common leg position in supine position. Knees are bent at 90 degrees and directly above the hips. Shins are parallel to the floor.

Zipping in the abs: A visual cue to pull in the abs as if zipping up a tight pair of jeans.

Full-Body Anatomy

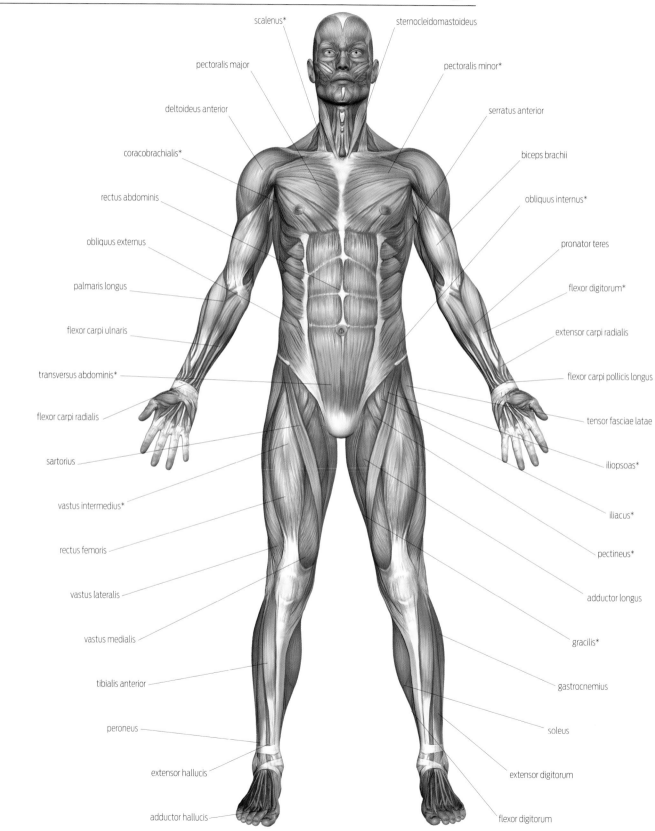

scalenus*

sternocleidomastoideus

pectoralis major

pectoralis minor*

deltoideus anterior

serratus anterior

coracobrachialis*

biceps brachii

rectus abdominis

obliquus internus*

obliquus externus

pronator teres

palmaris longus

flexor digitorum*

flexor carpi ulnaris

extensor carpi radialis

transversus abdominis*

flexor carpi pollicis longus

flexor carpi radialis

tensor fasciae latae

sartorius

iliopsoas*

vastus intermedius*

iliacus*

rectus femoris

pectineus*

vastus lateralis

adductor longus

vastus medialis

gracilis*

tibialis anterior

gastrocnemius

peroneus

soleus

extensor hallucis

extensor digitorum

adductor hallucis

flexor digitorum

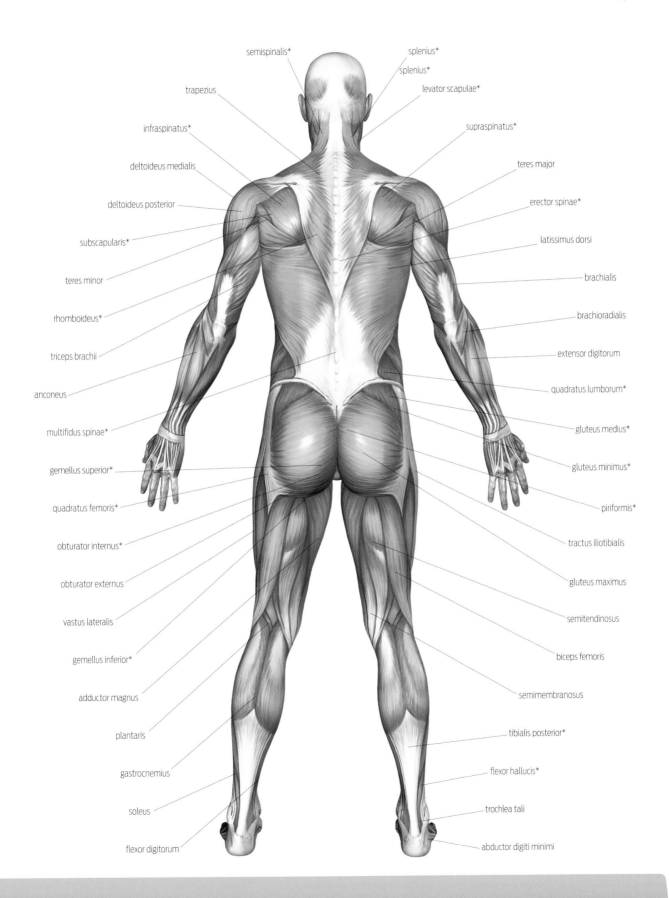

semispinalis*

splenius*

splenius*

trapezius

levator scapulae*

infraspinatus*

supraspinatus*

deltoideus medialis

teres major

deltoideus posterior

erector spinae*

subscapularis*

latissimus dorsi

teres minor

brachialis

rhomboideus*

brachioradialis

triceps brachii

extensor digitorum

anconeus

quadratus lumborum*

multifidus spinae*

gluteus medius*

gemellus superior*

gluteus minimus*

quadratus femoris*

piriformis*

obturator internus*

tractus iliotibialis

obturator externus

gluteus maximus

vastus lateralis

semitendinosus

gemellus inferior*

biceps femoris

adductor magnus

semimembranosus

plantaris

tibialis posterior*

gastrocnemius

flexor hallucis*

soleus

trochlea tali

flexor digitorum

abductor digiti minimi

CHAPTER ONE

Mat Work Exercises

Pilates mat exercises are an ideal way for you to get a low-impact workout while improving your posture, coordination, and balance. As you move through your mat work routine, try to isolate the muscles and joints involved in each movement and keep the rest of your body still. You'll become more aware of how your joints and muscles work in unison to create specific movements. Perform each exercise with fluid motions, flowing like a dancer from one step to the next. Focus on deep lateral breathing, which allows you to engage your abdominals throughout an exercise. Mindful breathing combined with precise, flowing movements during your workout will offer a deeper mind-body awareness and long-lasting health benefits. So roll out your mat and start working on your powerhouse!

"Patience and persistence are vital qualities in the ultimate successful accomplishment of any worthwhile endeavor."

—Joseph Pilates

001

Spine Stretch Forward

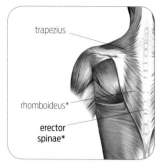

trapezius

rhomboideus*

erector spinae*

Correct form
Create a C-curve along your spine, from head to tailbone. Feel your ribcage expand outward as you inhale.

Avoid
Don't shift your pelvis or roll your knees inward.

The Spine Stretch Forward is a great beginner exercise that improves flexibility along the spine and in the hamstrings. As you perform this simple stretch, focus on articulating your spine as you slowly curl your body forward. Keep your abdominals engaged as you breathe laterally. If your hamstrings are tight, tuck a rolled-up towel under your hips and ease into the stretch.

Annotation Key
Bold text indicates target muscles
Black text indicates other working muscles
* indicates deep muscles

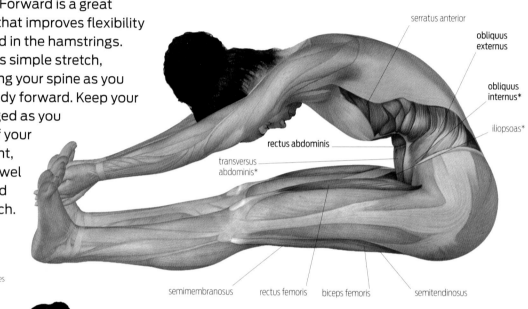

serratus anterior

obliquus externus

obliquus internus*

iliopsoas*

rectus abdominis

transversus abdominis*

semimembranosus   rectus femoris   biceps femoris   semitendinosus

- Sit upright with your legs extended in front of you. Position your feet about hip-width apart and flex your feet. Place your palms on the floor by your hips and inhale.

- Exhale as you curl forward, beginning with your head, neck, and upper back. Reach your arms forward, with palms facing up, and try to touch your feet. Hold for 30 seconds or longer.

- On exhale, slowly roll back to upright position.

002 Spine Stretch Reaching

This easy stretch is a great opportunity for you to practice pulling your shoulder blades down your back rather than hunching your shoulders and tensing your neck.

- Sit upright with legs forward and feet hip-width apart. Flex your feet. Raise your arms overhead, palms facing inward, and form a straight line with your back. Inhale to prepare.
- Exhale as you curl forward, reaching your arms forward at shoulder height. Hold for 30 seconds, breathing deeply.
- On an exhale, roll back to the starting position.

003 Spine Stretch Easier

Sit with your legs forward and knees bent. Place your feet flat on the floor, about hip-width apart. Rest your hands on the floor at your sides and inhale. Exhale as you curl your torso forward. Extend your arms along your shins, reaching your palms toward your feet. Hold for 30 seconds, breathing laterally. On an exhale, roll back to upright position.

004 Spine Stretch with Wide Legs

Sit with your legs forward. Flex your feet and position them more than hip-width apart. Place your palms on the floor at your sides and inhale. Exhale as you curl forward. Reach your arms forward, at shoulder height, and hold for 30 seconds. On an exhale, roll back to upright position.

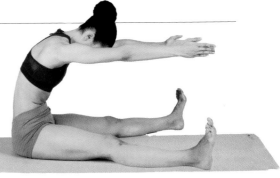

005

Saw

A classic Pilates exercise, the Saw uses oppositional movement to open the chest and upper back. The simultaneous twisting and curling of the torso improves spinal rotation and flexibility. The Saw also strengthens your obliques while stretching the spine, hamstrings, and hips. This is an excellent exercise to learn how to stabilize your pelvis during rotation.

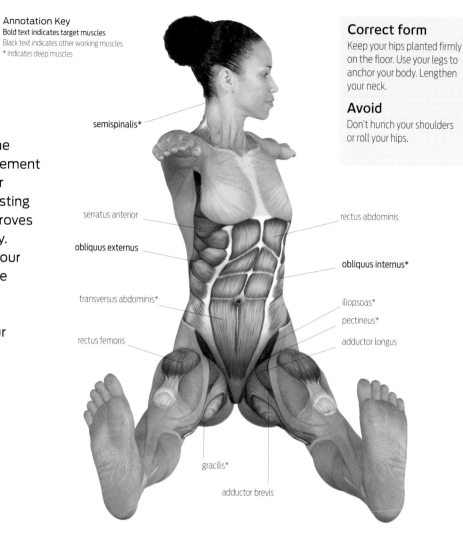

semispinalis*

serratus anterior

obliquus externus

transversus abdominis*

rectus femoris

rectus abdominis

obliquus internus*

iliopsoas*

pectineus*

adductor longus

gracilis*

adductor brevis

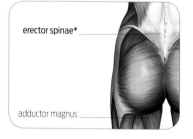

erector spinae*

adductor magnus

Correct form
Keep your hips planted firmly on the floor. Use your legs to anchor your body. Lengthen your neck.

Avoid
Don't hunch your shoulders or roll your hips.

- Sit upright and extend your legs forward. Flex your feet and position them more than hip-width apart.

- Raise your arms out to the sides, palms facing down. Inhale as you twist your torso to the left.

- Exhale as you reach your right hand over your left foot, as if "sawing" your little toe.

- Inhale and return to the starting position. Alternate sides and perform 5 repetitions per side.

006 Spine Twist Leg Lift on Ball

Take your twisting routine up a notch by balancing on a Swiss ball. Stabilize your hips and spine as you move through this exercise.

- Sit on a Swiss ball with your knees bent and your feet about shoulder-width apart. Plant your feet firmly on the floor.
- Inhale as you twist your torso to the right and raise your right leg to hip height. Flex your foot.
- Exhale as you return to the starting position. Focus on lengthening your spine and keeping it straight. Repeat 5 times on each side.

007 Spine Twist

In this simpler version of the Saw (#005), sit with your legs together and feet flexed. Extend your arms out to the sides. As you inhale and twist to the side, focus on rotating along your vertical axis. Keep your arms parallel to the floor. Repeat 5 times per side.

008 Spine Twist with Balls

Sit with your legs together and feet flexed. Hold a small weighted Pilates ball in each hand and perform the exercise as in the Spine Twist (#007). Begin with 3 repetitions per side.

009 Spine Twist with Band

Sit with legs together and feet flexed. Stretch a resistance band behind your back and hold the ends in each hand. Perform the exercise as in the Spine Twist (#007).

010 Saw with Arms Overhead

Sit with legs forward and feet flexed. Position your feet about hip-width apart. Extend your arms overhead and lengthen your spine. Complete the exercise as in the Saw (#005).

011

Curl-Up

The Curl-Up, also called the Crunch, is an essential Pilates exercise that strengthens your upper abdominals and stabilizes your core muscles. Master the Curl-Up with your hands clasped behind your head before moving on to the variations, so that you learn to articulate your spine using your abdominals rather than pulling up with your neck and shoulders.

Annotation Key
Bold text indicates target muscles
Black text indicates other working muscles
* indicates deep muscles

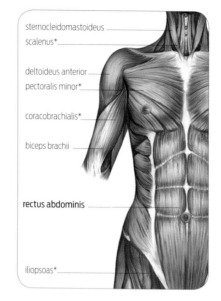

sternocleidomastoideus
scalenus*
deltoideus anterior
pectoralis minor*
coracobrachialis*
biceps brachii
rectus abdominis
iliopsoas*

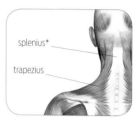

splenius*
trapezius

Correct form
Initiate the Curl-Up from your upper abs. The bottom of your shoulder blades should remain on the mat. Tuck your chin into your chest.

Avoid
Don't tense your neck or roll your elbows forward.

transversus abdominis*
obliquus externus
serratus anterior

- Lie on your back with your knees bent. Clasp your hands under your head for support.
- Keep your elbows wide, and behind your ears, and inhale deeply through your ribcage. As you begin to exhale, slowly curl your head, neck, and upper back from the mat.
- Inhale and roll back down, articulating your spine. Repeat 10 times.

012 Half Curl-Up

Lie on a mat with knees bent. Rest your arms at your sides and inhale. On exhale, slowly curl your head, neck, and shoulders off the mat. Extend your arms forward and parallel to the floor. Slowly roll down and repeat 10 times.

013 Tabletop Curl-Up

Lie on a mat with your feet on the floor. Lift your legs into tabletop position, so your knees are directly above your hips and your shins are parallel to the floor. Curl your head and shoulders from the mat and reach your arms forward.

014 Curl-Up with Swiss Ball

Lie on your back with your legs resting on a Swiss ball in tabletop position. Perform the exercise as in the Tabletop Curl-Up (#013).

015 Oblique Ankle Reach

Lie on a mat with knees bent and feet flat on the floor. Place your arms at your sides and inhale to prepare. Exhale, curl your head and shoulders off the mat, and lift your arms to shoulder height. Twist your torso to your left, reaching your left hand to your left heel. Lower on an exhale and alternate sides. Repeat 5 times per side.

016 Curl-Up on Roller

Lie on a mat with the middle of your back resting on a foam roller. Bend your knees and press your feet into the mat. Clasp your hands behind your head and inhale. As you exhale, curl your head and upper back off the mat. Roll down and repeat 5 times.

017 Oblique Curl-Up on Roller

Lie on a mat with the middle of your back on a foam roller. Bend your knees and press your feet into the mat. Clasp your hands behind your head and inhale. As you exhale, slowly curl up off the floor and twist to your left. Inhale and roll back down. Repeat 5 times per side.

018

Roll-Up

The Roll-Up requires significant powerhouse strength and controlled articulation of the spine. Beginners may have trouble lifting the back completely off the floor midway through the exercise. Be patient: Focus on pulling in your abdominals and curling your body up and over your navel. Try to lift one vertebra at a time in a fluid motion.

Correct form
Engage your abs and press your heels into the floor. If you're having difficulty, bend your knees slightly or place a rolled-up towel under your lower back.

Avoid
Don't wobble or swing up using momentum.

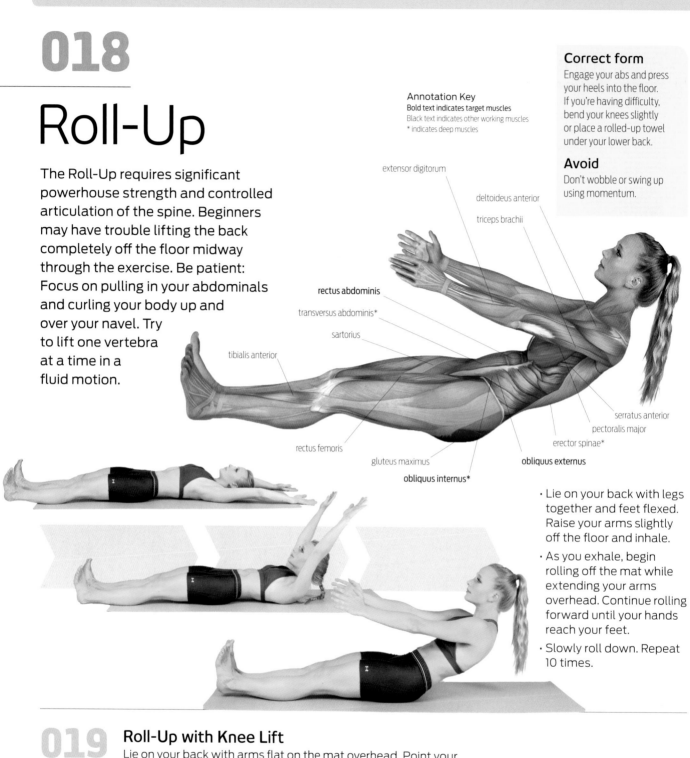

extensor digitorum

deltoideus anterior

triceps brachii

rectus abdominis

transversus abdominis*

sartorius

tibialis anterior

rectus femoris

gluteus maximus

obliquus internus*

serratus anterior

pectoralis major

erector spinae*

obliquus externus

- Lie on your back with legs together and feet flexed. Raise your arms slightly off the floor and inhale.
- As you exhale, begin rolling off the mat while extending your arms overhead. Continue rolling forward until your hands reach your feet.
- Slowly roll down. Repeat 10 times.

019 Roll-Up with Knee Lift

Lie on your back with arms flat on the mat overhead. Point your toes and raise your right leg into tabletop position. Curl up from the mat, reaching your arms forward. Keep your right knee bent as you lower your foot to the mat.
Repeat 5 times per leg.

020 Half Roll-Up with Twist

Lie on your back and extend your arms overhead on the mat. Bend your knees and raise your right leg into tabletop position. As you curl your head and shoulders off the mat, twist your torso and arms to the right. Repeat 5 times on each side.

021 Roll-Up with Ball

Lie flat on your back with legs together and feet flexed. Hold a small weighted ball and extend your arms overhead on the mat. Lift your arms up as you curl your head and neck off the floor. Continue rolling forward and touch the ball to your feet. Slowly roll back down. Repeat 5 times.

022 Roll-Up and Arm Press

Lie flat on your back with legs together and toes pointed. Hold a magic circle above your chest and extend your arms straight up. As you roll your head and neck off the floor, reach your arms forward and squeeze the circle. Roll back down to the starting position. Repeat 5 times.

023 Neck Pull

Lie flat on your back with legs together and feet flexed. Clasp your hands behind your head and keep your elbows wide. Roll up, slowly articulating your spine. Your back should form a C-curve as you touch your elbows to your knees. Roll down to the starting position. Repeat 5 times.

024

Half Roll-Back

The Half Roll-Back provides a solid core workout with less effort than the full Roll-Up. Paramount to the success of this exercise are the fundamental Pilates elements of articulating the spine and maintaining a strong C-curve with your back.

Correct form
Push your shoulders down and support your arms with your lat muscles. Control the movement from your core.

Avoid
Don't tense up your neck or shoulders.

deltoideus

obliquus externus

rectus abdominis

obliquus internus*

transversus abdominis*

tensor fasciae latae

sartorius

adductor magnus

gluteus maximus

teres major

latissimus dorsi

- Sit upright with legs together and knees bent. Extend your arms forward at shoulder height.
- Tuck your chin into your chest and inhale. On exhale, curl your spine into a C-curve and begin to roll down, scooping your abs and articulating your spine.
- Roll down until your lower back is touching the mat. Inhale and return to the sitting position. Repeat 10 times.

025 Half Roll-Back with Circle
Sit upright with a magic circle between your knees. Inhale and extend your arms forward at shoulder height. On exhale, squeeze the magic circle with your knees and roll down until your lower back touches the mat. Inhale as you return to the sitting position and release the tension on the circle. Repeat 5 times.

026 Half Roll-Back and Arm Press with Band

Sit upright with legs together and knees bent. Wrap a resistance band under your feet and hold the ends with both hands just above your knees. As you begin to roll down, pull your arms back and press your elbows outward. Return to the starting position and repeat 5 times.

027 Oblique Half Roll-Back

Sit upright with legs together and knees bent. Extend your arms out to the sides and parallel to the floor. As you roll down, scoop in your abs and twist your torso to the left. Keep your arms parallel to the floor and turn your gaze to the left. Return to the starting position and repeat 5 times on each side.

028 Oblique Half Roll-Back and Thigh Press

Sit upright with your knees bent. Place a magic circle between your knees and extend your arms forward. As you roll down, scoop in your abs and twist your torso and arms to the right. Return to the starting position and repeat 5 times on each side.

029 Climb the Tree

Lie on the floor with your knees bent. Raise your right leg straight up and place your hands behind your right thigh. As you curl off the floor, touch your hands progressively higher on your leg toward your ankle. Roll down and tap your hands downward along your leg. Repeat 5 times on each leg.

030 Climb the Tree, Leg Pulses

Lie on the floor with your knees bent. Raise your left leg straight up and place your hands behind your ankle. Gently pull your leg toward your torso and pulse several times. Repeat 5 times on each leg.

031

Butterfly Stretch

Keep your inner thighs limber with the Butterfly Stretch. This exercise targets the adductor muscles and improves mobility in the hip joints. Flexible adductors are essential for any activity that requires hip rotation or side-to-side agility. These muscles also help stabilize the knees. The Butterfly is an ideal stretch to perform after lunges.

gracilis*

adductor longus

adductor brevis

pectineus*

- Sit upright with knees bent and the soles of your feet together. Try to tuck your heels as close to your groin as possible. Place your hands on your ankles and inhale.

- As you exhale, press your knees into the floor and bend your body forward from your hips, leaning over your legs.

- Hold for 30 seconds, breathing deeply. On an inhale, return to the starting position.

032 Cross-Legged Forward Reach

Sit upright with your legs comfortably crossed, first with your left foot over the right. Rest your hands on your knees, lengthen your spine, and inhale. Slowly exhale and walk your hands forward, articulating your spine. Hold for up to 30 seconds and gently return to sitting position. Repeat with your right foot crossing the left.

033 Cross-Legged Diagonal Reach

Sit upright with your legs comfortably crossed. Extend your arms overhead and inhale. Slowly curl your torso forward and twist diagonally to your left, touching your palms to the floor. Hold for 20 seconds and repeat to the opposite side.

034 Cross-Legged Side Stretch

Sit upright with your legs comfortably crossed. Extend your arms overhead, palms facing inward, and inhale. Slowly bend to your left as you exhale, and rest your left forearm at your side. Extend your right arm overhead. Breathe slowly and deeply for 20 seconds and repeat to the opposite side.

035 Cross-Legged Roll-Down

Sit upright with your legs comfortably crossed. Place your hands on your knees, lengthen your spine, and inhale. Curl forward, articulating your spine, as you exhale. Relax your shoulders and hold for 30 seconds.

036 Cross-Legged Side Bend with Band

Sit upright with your legs comfortably crossed. Stretch a resistance band overhead, holding the ends in each hand, and inhale to prepare. As you exhale, bend to your left and stretch the band down to the floor with your left hand. Hold for 20 seconds and alternate sides.

037

Rising Swan

The backward extension of the Rising Swan opens your chest, abdominals, and hip flexors. This exercise offers your back a nice counter-stretch after performing forward flexion exercises. It's also a relaxing stretch after a long day of sitting in a chair. To get the most benefit from the Rising Swan, focus on lengthening your spine and engaging the powerhouse muscles in your lower back and abs to lift your upper body from the mat.

Correct form
Pull your chest forward and upward and elongate your neck and spine.

Avoid
Don't attempt to lift your torso so high that you crunch your spine. Do not rely solely on your hands to push through the movement.

trapezius

teres major

latissimus dorsi

quadratus lumborum*

gluteus maximus

biceps femoris

deltoideus

biceps brachii

brachialis

rectus lateralis   rectus femoris   tensor fasciae latae   triceps brachii

- Lie facedown on a mat with your legs and heels pressed together. Bend your arms in at your sides and place your palms by your ears.

- Squeeze your inner thighs and buttocks and pull your navel into your spine. Inhale as you press your forearms, pubic bone, and feet into the mat. Slowly peel your torso off the mat.

- Hold for 20 seconds and repeat 3 times.

038 Swan

Lie facedown on a mat with your legs and heels pressed together. Bend your arms in at your sides and place your palms by your shoulders. Inhale as you push your pubic bone, thighs, and feet into the mat and raise your torso, lifting up onto your hands. Hold for 20 seconds and repeat 5 times.

039 Swan with Ball

Lie facedown on a mat. Extend your arms overhead and rest your hands on a medium ball. Inhale and push your pubic bone, thighs, and feet into the mat. Slowly peel your chest and abdomen up from the mat. Hold for 20 seconds and repeat 5 times.

040 Arch-Ups on Swiss Ball

The Swiss ball provides a cushion for your lower torso yet adds a degree of difficulty in stabilizing your hips and spine. If you find that you're rolling backward, support your feet against a wall or a table. Control the movement and avoid hyperextending your lower back.

- Position your hips over the Swiss ball. Press your palms into the floor and inhale.
- Find your balance and peel your chest from the ball as you exhale.
- Extend your arms out to the sides, pressing your shoulder blades together while lengthening your spine.
- Hold for 20 seconds.

041

Hundred 1

A classic Pilates exercise, the Hundred 1 is a great abdominal workout that's deceptively challenging. You need to stabilize your core while coordinating your breathing pattern with your arm pulses. You may need to work your way up to the full 100 pulses, but you'll be strengthening your powerhouse along the way.

Annotation Key
Bold text indicates target muscles
Black text indicates other working muscles
* indicates deep muscles

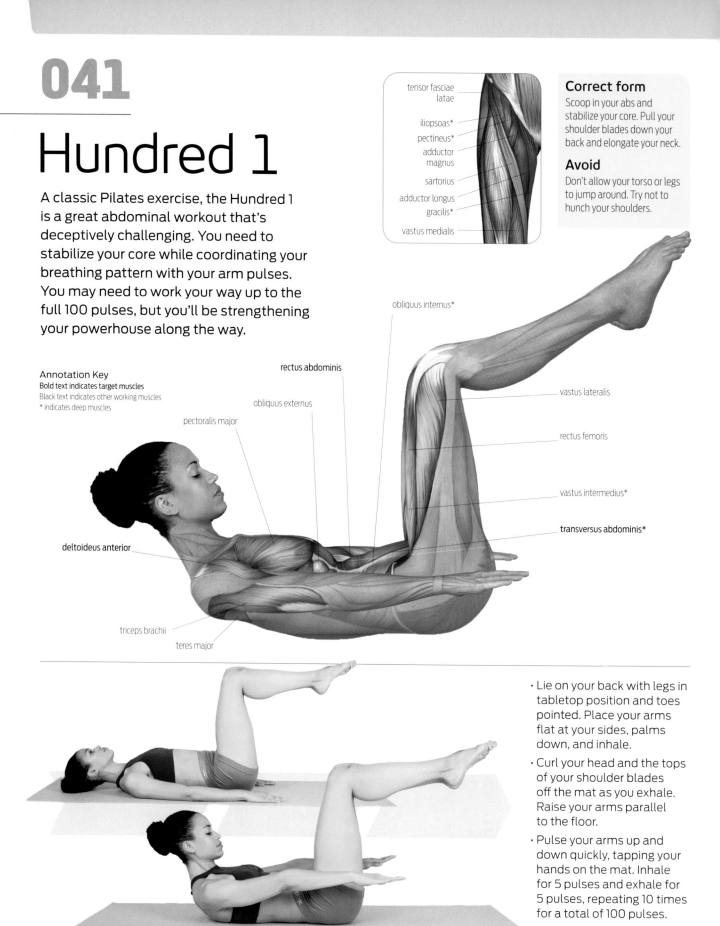

tensor fasciae latae

iliopsoas*

pectineus*

adductor magnus

sartorius

adductor longus

gracilis*

vastus medialis

Correct form
Scoop in your abs and stabilize your core. Pull your shoulder blades down your back and elongate your neck.

Avoid
Don't allow your torso or legs to jump around. Try not to hunch your shoulders.

obliquus internus*

rectus abdominis

obliquus externus

pectoralis major

vastus lateralis

rectus femoris

vastus intermedius*

transversus abdominis*

deltoideus anterior

triceps brachii

teres major

- Lie on your back with legs in tabletop position and toes pointed. Place your arms flat at your sides, palms down, and inhale.

- Curl your head and the tops of your shoulder blades off the mat as you exhale. Raise your arms parallel to the floor.

- Pulse your arms up and down quickly, tapping your hands on the mat. Inhale for 5 pulses and exhale for 5 pulses, repeating 10 times for a total of 100 pulses.

042 Hundred 1 Prep

Lie on your back with knees bent and feet on the floor. Place your arms flat at your sides, palms down, and inhale. Curl your head and the tops of your shoulder blades off the mat on exhale. Perform the exercise as in the Hundred 1 (#041).

043 Hundred 1 Tiptoes

Lie on your back with knees bent and feet on the mat. Place your arms at your sides, palms down. Lift your feet onto tiptoes and inhale. Perform the exercise as in the Hundred 1 (#041).

044 Single-Leg Hundred 1

Lie on your back with knees bent and feet on the mat. Place your arms at your sides, palms down. Lift your left leg into tabletop, flexing the foot. Keep your left leg raised while you complete the exercise as in the Hundred 1 (#041). Repeat on the opposite leg.

045 Hundred 1 with Band

Add a resistance band to your Hundred workout to challenge your arm and shoulder muscles. It's also an excellent exercise to improve your coordination.

- Lie on your back with legs in tabletop position. Wrap a resistance band around your shins and hold the ends in either hand.
- As you pulse your arms and pull down on the band, you engage more muscles in the arms and shoulders. Perform the exercise as in the Hundred 1 (#041).

046

Hundred 2

Once you've mastered the Hundred 1, you're ready to take it to the next level with the Hundred 2. This advanced version develops leg strength while challenging your powerhouse. The Hundred 2 gets your circulation going and really develops your core muscle endurance.

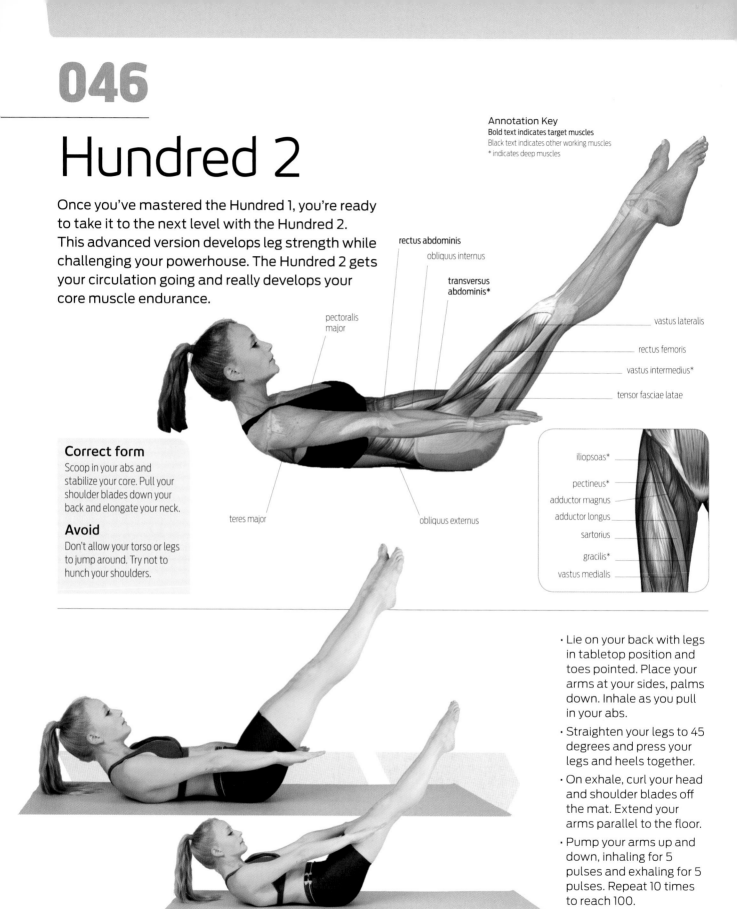

rectus abdominis
obliquus internus
transversus abdominis*
pectoralis major

vastus lateralis
rectus femoris
vastus intermedius*
tensor fasciae latae

iliopsoas*
pectineus*
adductor magnus
adductor longus
sartorius
gracilis*
vastus medialis

teres major
obliquus externus

Correct form
Scoop in your abs and stabilize your core. Pull your shoulder blades down your back and elongate your neck.

Avoid
Don't allow your torso or legs to jump around. Try not to hunch your shoulders.

- Lie on your back with legs in tabletop position and toes pointed. Place your arms at your sides, palms down. Inhale as you pull in your abs.
- Straighten your legs to 45 degrees and press your legs and heels together.
- On exhale, curl your head and shoulder blades off the mat. Extend your arms parallel to the floor.
- Pump your arms up and down, inhaling for 5 pulses and exhaling for 5 pulses. Repeat 10 times to reach 100.

047 Hundred 2 Ankle Press with Circle

Ramp up the resistance! Boost your coordination and stamina with a magic circle or a Pilates ball.

- Lie on your back with legs in tabletop position and balance a magic circle between your ankles. Place your arms at your sides and inhale.
- Extend your legs to 45 degrees and squeeze the circle.
- On exhale, curl your head and shoulder blades off the floor and raise your arms to shoulder height.
- Pump your arms up and down, inhaling for 5 pulses and exhaling for 5 pulses. Repeat 10 times for 100 pulses.

048 Hundred 2 with Ball at Ankles

Lie on your back with legs in tabletop position and balance a medium Pilates ball between your ankles. Place your arms at your sides and inhale. Extend your legs to 45 degrees and squeeze the ball. Perform as in the Hundred 2 (#046).

049 Hundred 2 with Ball at Knees

Lie on your back with legs in tabletop position and balance a medium Pilates ball between your knees. Place your arms at your sides and inhale. Extend your legs to 45 degrees and squeeze the ball. Perform as in the Hundred 2 (#046).

050 Hundred 2 with Legs Upward

Lie on your back with your legs in tabletop position and toes pointed. Place your arms flat at your sides, palms down. Inhale and raise your legs to 90 degrees. Perform as in the Hundred 2 (#046). As your strength improves, gradually lower your legs until you are able to hold them at 45 degrees.

051
Rollover

This demanding Pilates exercise requires a strong core and a controlled, fluid progression. With time and practice, you can perfect this advanced exercise by fully engaging your abs, articulating your spine, and breathing deeply. Flex your feet to stretch your hamstrings and calves and feel the energy release through your heels.

Correct form
If you're having difficulty rolling over, bend your knees slightly or place a rolled-up towel under your hips.

Avoid
Don't use momentum to push through the movement.

rectus abdominis
obliquus internus*
transversus *abdominis
tensor fasciae latae
iliopsoas
pectineus
sartorius
adductor longus
rectus femoris

gluteus maximus
gluteus medius*
gluteus minimus
obliquus externus
latissimus dorsi
teres major

adductor magnus
gracilis*
gastrocnemius
soleus

deltoideus posterior

Annotation Key
Bold text indicates target muscles
Black text indicates other working muscles
* indicates deep muscles

- Lie on your back with knees bent and arms at your sides. Inhale and elongate your spine.
- On exhale, raise your legs straight up and squeeze them together.
- Peel your spine off the mat and press into your palms for stability as you pull your legs overhead, parallel to the floor. Roll down slowly. Repeat 5 times.

052
Rollover Ankle Press with Ball
Lie on your back with knees bent and arms at your sides. Balance a medium Pilates ball between your ankles and inhale. Engage your lower abs and elongate your neck and spine. On exhale, raise your legs to 90 degrees, squeezing the ball. Complete the exercise as in the Rollover (#051).

053 Rollover Ankle Press with Circle

Lie on your back with knees bent and arms at your sides. Balance a magic circle between your ankles and inhale. Engage your lower abs and elongate your neck and spine. As you exhale, raise your legs to 90 degrees, squeezing the circle. Perform as in the Rollover (#051).

054 Reverse Curl

Lie on your back with knees bent and feet hip-width apart. Place your arms at your sides and inhale. Lift your feet off the floor. Exhale as you peel your back off the floor, tucking your knees into your chest. Return to the starting position and repeat 5 times.

055 Reverse Curl with Ball

Lie on your back with knees bent and feet hip-width apart. Rest your arms at your sides and inhale. Place a medium Pilates ball between your knees and perform the exercise as in Reverse Curl (#054).

056 Control Balance

Lie on your back with legs straight up and arms at your sides. Inhale and engage your abs. On exhale, peel your spine off the mat and lower your legs overhead, parallel to the floor. Swing your arms around to hold your right foot. Straighten your left leg toward the ceiling. Alternate legs and repeat for 5 sets.

057 Jackknife

Lie on your back with legs straight up and arms at your sides. Inhale and engage your abs. As you exhale, peel your spine off the mat and lower your legs parallel to the floor. Use your powerhouse to lift your legs into a 45-degree angle. Perform 5 repetitions.

058 Boomerang

Sit with legs forward and ankles crossed. Place your hands near your ankles. Roll backward, lowering your legs parallel to the floor. Cross your ankles in the other direction and roll forward into Teaser. Clasp your hands behind your back and lower your head to your knees. Bring your arms forward and stretch.

059

Rolling Like a Ball

The dynamic rocking motion of Rolling Like a Ball massages your spine and increases circulation along your back. This is one of the few Pilates exercises that relies on momentum to propel you through a movement. To perform Rolling Like a Ball smoothly, concentrate on finding your balance and use your abdominals to control the motion from start to finish.

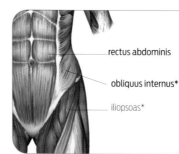

rectus abdominis

obliquus internus*

iliopsoas*

Correct form
Roll only until your shoulder blades touch the mat. Try to keep your knees bent at 90 degrees throughout.

Avoid
Don't roll onto your neck or hunch your shoulders.

Annotation Key
Bold text indicates target muscles
Black text indicates other working muscles
* indicates deep muscles

transversus abdominis*

obliquus externus

gluteus maximus

gluteus minimus*

gluteus medius*

- Sit upright with knees bent and legs together.
- Clasp your hands around your shins, or hold the backs of your thighs, and scoop in your abs as much as you are able.
- Lift one foot off the floor at a time, inhale, and roll backward.
- Exhale and roll forward. Repeat 5 times.

060 Roll-Down

Sit with knees bent and feet flat on a mat. Extend your arms forward and inhale. Scoop your abs and form a C-curve along your spine. Exhale and roll your lower and middle back to the mat. Keep your arms parallel to the floor. Return to the starting position and repeat 10 times.

061 Pike Roll

Sit upright with knees bent and legs together. Extend one leg at a time to 45 degrees, place your hands under your calves, and inhale. Roll backward, just to the bottom of your shoulder blades, and exhale. Roll to the starting position and repeat 5 times.

062 Crab Roll

Sit upright with knees bent. Cross your lower legs and hold the top of each ankle with the opposite hand. Raise your feet off the floor and inhale, balancing on your hips. On exhale, roll backward, to the bottom of your shoulder blades. Roll to the starting position and repeat 5 times.

063 Rolling Ankle Press

Squeeze a Pilates ball between your ankles to engage your deep abdominal muscles. Rolling exercises are great for releasing tension in the back as the rocking motion massages the spine.

- Sit upright with your legs forward. Place a medium Pilates ball between your ankles and inhale.

- Begin scooping your abs as you roll backward into Teaser. Keep your arms extended in front of you as you exhale. Continue rolling back in a smooth motion until your legs are parallel to the floor.

- Squeeze the ball throughout. Inhale and roll forward. Repeat 5 times.

064 Open-Leg Rocker

The Open-Leg Rocker works the abdominals like other Pilates rolling exercises, but this exercise also strengthens the latissimus dorsi muscles along the sides of the back.

- Sit upright with your feet shoulder-width apart and legs straight.
- Lift your legs to 45 degrees and place your hands on your calves.
- Inhale and roll onto your lower and middle back, keeping your head and shoulders off the mat.
- Exhale and roll to the starting position. Repeat 5 times.

065 Seal

Sit upright with knees bent. Reach between your thighs and wrap your hands around the outside of your ankles. Raise your feet off the floor with your knees at a 90-degree angle. Inhale and balance on your hips. Roll backward, down to the bottom of your shoulder blades. Exhale and roll to the starting position. Hold briefly and repeat 5 times.

066 Rocker Straddle

Sit upright with your knees tucked into your chest and hold your ankles. Balance on your hips and scoop in your abdominals. Inhale and roll backward onto your shoulder blades. Exhale as you roll forward and open your legs into the straddle position. Repeat 5 times.

067 Rocking V-Sit

Sit upright with your knees tucked into your chest. Balance on your hips and scoop in your abdominals. Inhale and roll backward onto your shoulder blades. Exhale as you roll forward and extend your arms and legs into the V-position. Hold briefly and repeat 5 times.

068

Single-Leg Stretch

The Single-Leg Stretch is one of the dynamic exercises in the Pilates Stomach Series. It involves quick controlled arm and leg movements while keeping the core muscles stable.

rectus femoris

trapezius

serratus anterior

semimembranosus

biceps femoris

semitendinosus

gluteus maximus

rhomboideus*

latissimus dorsi

rectus abdominis

multifidus spinae*

quadratus lumborum*

obliquus externus

transversus abdominis*

obliquus internus*

Annotation Key
Bold text indicates target muscles
Black text indicates other working muscles
* indicates deep muscles

- Lie on your back with legs in tabletop and feet flexed. Place your arms at your sides.

- Inhale and curl your head and neck off the mat, reaching your hands to your shins.

- Exhale and extend your right leg to 45 degrees. Touch your left hand to your left ankle.

- Inhale as you begin to alternate legs. Exhale as you straighten your left leg and touch your right hand to your right ankle. Repeat 5 times on each side.

069 Single-Leg Stretch, Easier

Lie on your back with legs in tabletop position and feet flexed. Place your arms at your sides. Inhale as you reach your hands to your calves. Perform the exercise as in the Single-Leg Stretch (#068).

070 Bent-Knee Hamstring Stretch

Lie on your back with legs flat on the floor and arms at your sides. Inhale and scoop in your abdominals as you bend your right knee. Exhale and press your knee into your chest. Hold the stretch for 30 seconds and repeat on the opposite leg.

071 Single-Leg Hamstring Stretch

Lie on your back with legs flat on the floor and arms at your sides. Inhale and scoop in your abs as you bend your right knee. Exhale, straighten your leg, and extend it toward the ceiling. Place your hands on your calf and gently pull your leg toward your chest. Hold the stretch for 30 seconds. Repeat on the opposite leg.

072 Single-Leg Hamstring Stretch with Band

Lie on your back with knees bent. Wrap a resistance band around your right foot. Inhale and extend your right leg toward the ceiling. Exhale and pull on the band to stretch your hamstrings. Hold for 30 seconds and repeat on the opposite leg.

073 Tiny Steps

Tiny Steps is an easier version of the Single-Leg Stretch (#068). By keeping your hands on your abdominals during the movement, you can feel whether you are engaging your abs and keeping your hips stable.

- Lie on your back with your knees bent and hands on your abdomen. Lift your feet onto tiptoes and inhale to prepare.
- Exhale and bend your left knee into your chest. Inhale as you begin to alternate legs, and exhale as your left toes touch the floor.
- Continue alternating legs for 10 sets.

074 Outer-Thigh Stretch with Band

Lie on your back with legs flat on the floor. Bend your right knee and wrap a resistance band around your right foot. Hold the band in your left hand. Inhale and extend your leg toward the ceiling. Exhale, cross your right leg over the left hip, and pull on the band. Hold for 30 seconds and repeat on the opposite leg.

075 Inner-Thigh Stretch with Band

Lie on your back with knees bent. Place a magic circle around your left foot and hold the ring with your left hand. Inhale and straighten your left leg. Press your right arm into the floor for balance. Exhale and pull on the circle to feel the stretch in your inner thigh. Hold for 20 seconds and repeat on the opposite leg.

076 Oblique Leg Stretch with Ball

Lie on your back with legs in tabletop position and feet flexed. Hold a small Pilates ball overhead. Inhale and curl your head and neck off the mat. Exhale and extend the ball toward your left side while straightening your right leg to 45 degrees. Inhale as you begin to alternate legs, and exhale as you straighten your left leg and twist your torso to your right. Continue alternating sides for 5 sets.

077 Piriformis Stretch with Band

Lie on your back with legs in tabletop position. Cross your left ankle over your right thigh and wrap a resistance band around your right foot. Pull on the band to stretch your piriformis. Hold for 30 seconds and alternate sides.

078 Piriformis Stretch with Circle

Lie on your back with legs in tabletop position. Cross your right ankle over your left thigh and place a magic circle around your left foot. Pull on the ring to stretch your piriformis. Hold for 30 seconds and alternate sides.

079

Leg Drops

Leg Drops strengthen the lower and middle abdominals to give you those six-pack abs. This exercise also helps stabilize your pelvis and spine. Think about the Pilates principles of control and precision as you slowly lower and raise your legs. If Leg Drops are difficult for you at first, tuck your hands under your hips for support or bend your knees slightly.

Correct form
Keep your back stable and pull in your abdominals. Press your torso and hips firmly into the mat.

Avoid
Don't arch your back or swing your legs.

sartorius

vastus medialis

adductor longus

rectus femoris

transversus abdominis*

rectus abdominis

gracilis*

semimembranosus

biceps femoris

vastus lateralis

soleus

gastrocnemius

tensor fasciae latae

semitendinosus

gluteus maximus

obliquus internus*

obliquus externus

iliopsoas*

pectineus*

Annotation Key
Bold text indicates target muscles
Black text indicates other working muscles
* indicates deep muscles

· Lie on your back with knees bent and arms at your sides. Raise your legs straight up, flexing your feet, and inhale.

· Scoop in your abs and exhale as you lower your right leg to 45 degrees from the floor. Keep your hips firmly grounded.

· Return your right leg to the upright position and alternate legs for 10 sets.

080 Double-Leg Drops

Lie on your back with legs straight up and feet flexed. Place your arms at your sides and inhale. Pull your navel into your spine and exhale as you slowly lower your legs to 45 degrees from the floor. Keep your hips firmly planted into the mat. Repeat 10 times.

081 Double Dips with Ball
Lie on your back and place a medium Pilates ball between your ankles. Extend your legs straight up and flex your feet. Place your arms at your sides and inhale. Engage your abs and exhale as you slowly lower your legs to 45 degrees. Return your legs to the upright position and repeat 10 times.

082 Leg Drops to Sides
Lie on your back with legs extended upward. Flex your feet, press your heels together, and turn out your toes in the Pilates V. Place your arms at your sides and inhale. Exhale as you slowly lower your legs out to the sides. Try to lengthen your legs and lift them from the hip joints. Return to the upright position and repeat 10 times.

083 Criss-Cross
Lie on your back with legs extended upward and cross your ankles. Place your arms at your sides, pull your navel to your spine, and inhale. Exhale and slowly lower your legs to 45 degrees, criss-crossing your ankles front and back. Keep your hips stable. Return to the upright position and repeat 10 times.

084 Double Dips with Circle
Lie on your back and place a magic circle between your ankles. Extend your legs upward, clasp your hands behind your head, and inhale. Pull your navel to your spine and exhale as you slowly lower your legs to 45 degrees. Squeeze the circle and keep your hips stable. Return your legs to the upright position and repeat 10 times.

085 Double-Leg Lowers, Supported
Lie on your back and prop yourself up on your forearms. Raise your legs straight up, pointing your toes, and inhale. Pull your navel to your spine. Exhale as you slowly lower your legs to 45 degrees. Return your legs to the upright position and repeat 10 times.

086 Diagonal Leg Lowers with Ball
Lie on your back and place a medium Pilates ball between your ankles. Prop yourself up on your forearms and extend your legs straight up. Twist and lower your legs to your right. Return your legs to the upright position and repeat to the opposite side for 5 sets.

087

Leg Circles

Leg Circles improve your pelvic stability and develop the deep muscles of your pelvic floor. This exercise strengthens your core, quadriceps, and hamstrings. Try to envision lengthening the raised leg and pulling it out from your psoas muscles, the largest of the hip flexors that connect your lower spine to your inner thighs.

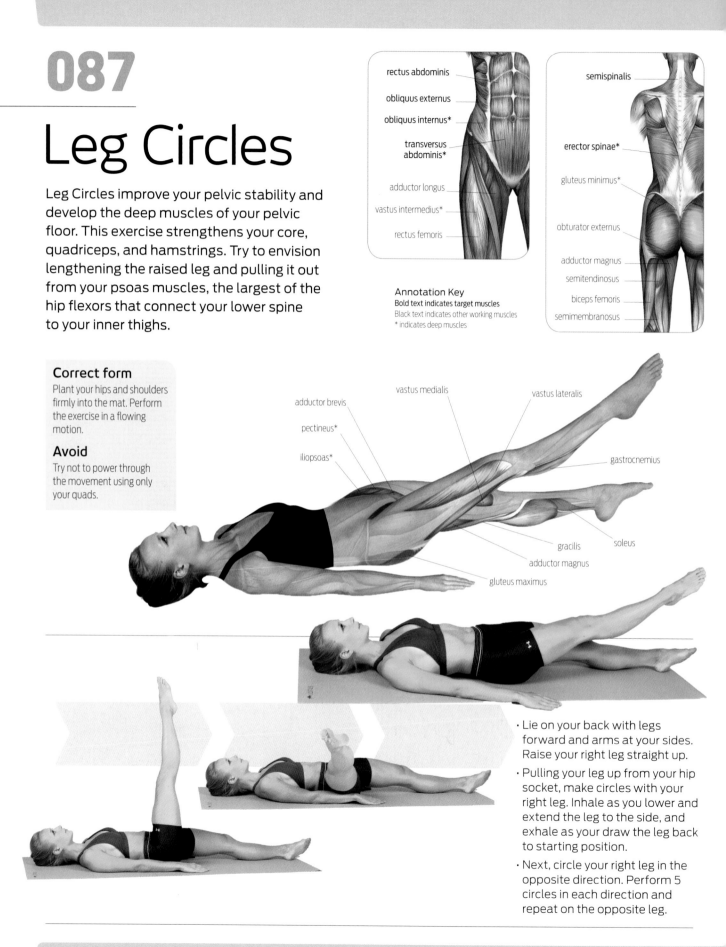

rectus abdominis
obliquus externus
obliquus internus*
transversus abdominis*
adductor longus
vastus intermedius*
rectus femoris

semispinalis
erector spinae*
gluteus minimus*
obturator externus
adductor magnus
semitendinosus
biceps femoris
semimembranosus

Annotation Key
Bold text indicates target muscles
Black text indicates other working muscles
* indicates deep muscles

Correct form
Plant your hips and shoulders firmly into the mat. Perform the exercise in a flowing motion.

Avoid
Try not to power through the movement using only your quads.

vastus medialis
adductor brevis
pectineus*
iliopsoas*
vastus lateralis
gastrocnemius
gracilis
soleus
adductor magnus
gluteus maximus

- Lie on your back with legs forward and arms at your sides. Raise your right leg straight up.

- Pulling your leg up from your hip socket, make circles with your right leg. Inhale as you lower and extend the leg to the side, and exhale as your draw the leg back to starting position.

- Next, circle your right leg in the opposite direction. Perform 5 circles in each direction and repeat on the opposite leg.

088 Single-Leg Circles, Easier
Lie on your back with legs forward and arms at your sides. Bend your left knee and raise your right leg straight up. Perform the exercise as in Leg Circles (#087).

089 Single-Knee Circles
Lie on your back with legs forward and arms at your sides. Bend your right knee into your chest. Place your right hand on your knee and gently make clockwise circles, rotating your leg around your hip socket. Circle your knee in the opposite direction. Perform 5 circles in each direction and repeat on the opposite leg.

090 Double-Leg Circles
Lie on your back with legs pointing upward. Clasp your hands behind your head and inhale. Pull your navel to your spine and curl your head and neck off the mat. Exhale as you lower your legs out to the sides, pulling them up from the hip sockets. Continue circling down and back to the middle. Repeat the circles in the opposite direction for 5 sets.

091 Double-Leg Circles, Supported
Lie on your back and prop yourself up on your forearms. Extend your legs straight up and inhale to prepare. Exhale as you lower your legs out to the sides, pulling them up from the hip sockets. Continue circling down and back to the middle. Repeat the circles in the opposite direction for 5 sets.

092 Alternating Leg Lifts on Foam Roller
Position a foam roller under your back and bend your knees. Extend your arms out to the sides. Raise your left leg into tabletop position and inhale. Draw small, controlled circles around your left hip for 20 seconds. Work toward raising your arms off the floor. Lower your left foot and repeat on the opposite leg for 5 sets.

093 Hip Flexor Stretch on Foam Roller
Place a foam roller under your sacrum. Bend your knees and extend your arms out to the sides. Bring your left knee into your chest and lower your right foot to the floor. Form small circles with your left leg for 20 seconds. Repeat on the opposite leg.

094

Scissors

A classic Pilates exercise, Scissors targets your abdominals and hamstrings and builds stamina. Apply the principles of precision, control, and flow to benefit fully from the exercise. As you gain confidence and can maintain a steady rhythm, try to release energy from your hips and out through your pointed toes.

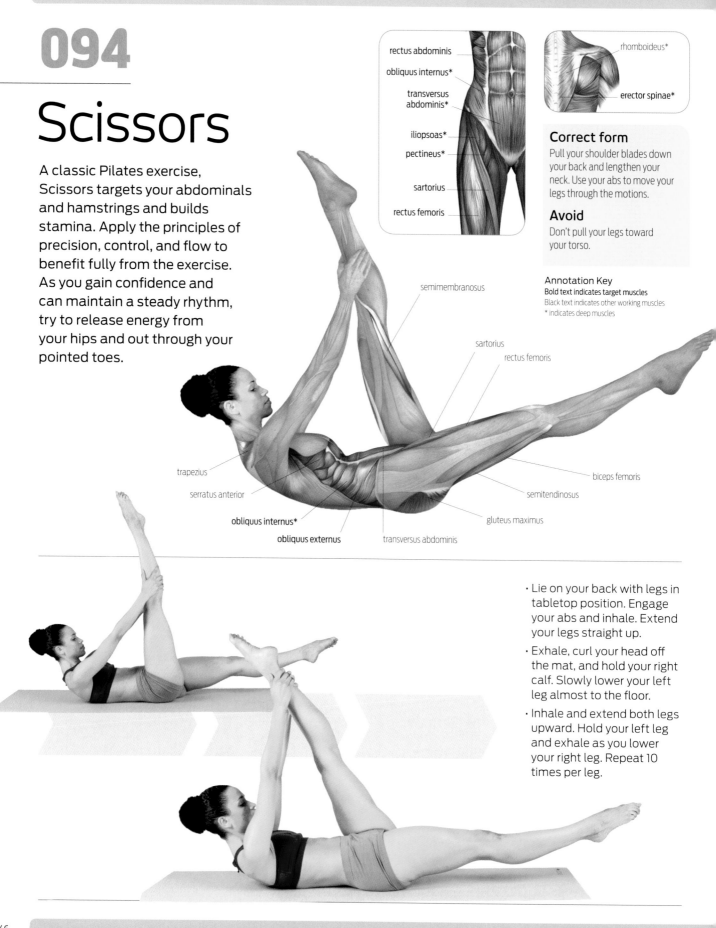

rectus abdominis

obliquus internus*

transversus abdominis*

iliopsoas*

pectineus*

sartorius

rectus femoris

rhomboideus*

erector spinae*

Correct form
Pull your shoulder blades down your back and lengthen your neck. Use your abs to move your legs through the motions.

Avoid
Don't pull your legs toward your torso.

Annotation Key
Bold text indicates target muscles
Black text indicates other working muscles
* indicates deep muscles

semimembranosus

sartorius

rectus femoris

trapezius

serratus anterior

obliquus internus*

obliquus externus

transversus abdominis

gluteus maximus

biceps femoris

semitendinosus

- Lie on your back with legs in tabletop position. Engage your abs and inhale. Extend your legs straight up.
- Exhale, curl your head off the mat, and hold your right calf. Slowly lower your left leg almost to the floor.
- Inhale and extend both legs upward. Hold your left leg and exhale as you lower your right leg. Repeat 10 times per leg.

095 Scissors Supported

Lie on your back with legs straight and toes pointed. Prop yourself up on your forearms. Pull your navel into your spine and inhale. Extend your legs toward the ceiling. Exhale and slowly lower your right leg almost to the floor. Inhale and bring both legs to 90 degrees. Exhale and lower your left leg. Repeat 10 times with each leg.

096 Scissors on Balance Ball

Lie on a balance ball, supporting your middle back on the dome. As you inhale, extend both legs toward the ceiling and reach your hands to your right calf. Exhale and slowly lower your left leg parallel to the floor. Inhale, bring both legs to 90 degrees, and hold your left calf. Exhale as you lower your right leg. Repeat 10 times per leg.

097 Scissors on Roller

Lie on a mat with a foam roller under your sacrum. Inhale, extend your legs toward the ceiling, and place your arms out to the sides. Exhale and lower your right leg parallel to the floor. Inhale and bring both legs to 90 degrees. Alternate legs and repeat 10 sets.

098 Bicycle Twist

Lie on your back with legs in tabletop. Clasp your hands behind your head and curl your head from the mat. Twist to the right as you extend your left leg to 45 degrees. Touch your left elbow to your right knee as you exhale. Alternate sides in a fluid motion. Perform 5 sets.

099 High Bicycle

Lie on your back with legs in tabletop position and hands at your sides. Pull your legs toward the ceiling and place your hands on your hips for balance. Straighten your right leg overhead while bending your left knee. Pedal your legs in a continuous movement for 30 seconds.

100

Double-Leg Stretch

The Double-Leg Stretch is an excellent workout for your abdominals, particularly the obliques and transverse muscles. Keep in mind that the lower you extend your arms and legs, the greater the level of difficulty. Begin by extending your arms and legs higher than 45 degrees in a smooth, controlled manner.

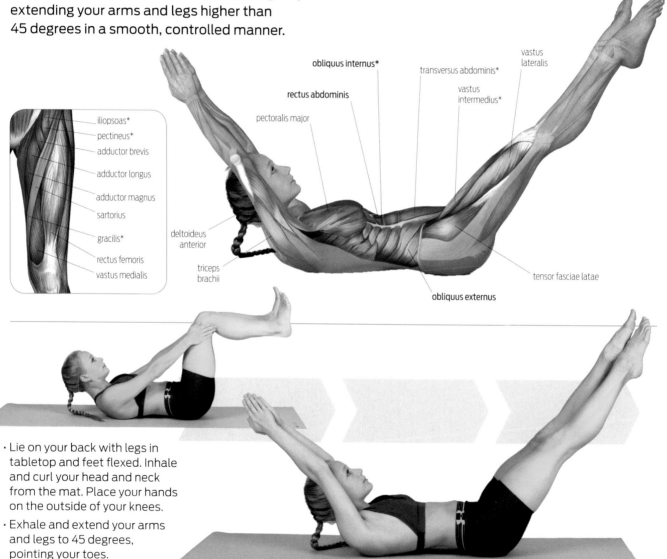

iliopsoas*
pectineus*
adductor brevis
adductor longus
adductor magnus
sartorius
gracilis*
rectus femoris
vastus medialis

obliquus internus*
rectus abdominis
pectoralis major
transversus abdominis*
vastus intermedius*
vastus lateralis
deltoideus anterior
triceps brachii
obliquus externus
tensor fasciae latae

- Lie on your back with legs in tabletop and feet flexed. Inhale and curl your head and neck from the mat. Place your hands on the outside of your knees.

- Exhale and extend your arms and legs to 45 degrees, pointing your toes.

- Inhale, return your legs to tabletop, and circle your arms out to the sides and back to your knees. Repeat 10 times.

101 Double-Leg Stretch Prep
Lie on your back and bring your knees into your chest. Place your hands on your ankles. Inhale and curl your head and neck from the mat. On exhale, raise your legs to 45 degrees and extend your arms in line with your torso. Perform 10 repetitions.

102 Double-Leg Stretch with Circle
Begin in tabletop position and balance a magic circle between your thighs. Squeeze the circle with your inner thighs and perform the exercise as in Double-Leg Stretch (#100).

103 Double-Leg Press with Band
Begin in tabletop position with a resistance band wrapped around your feet. Hold the ends of the band, supporting your elbows on the mat. As you exhale, push your legs out to 45 degrees. Inhale and return to the starting position. Repeat 10 times.

104 Double-Leg Press and Crunch on Balance Ball

The balance ball may look simple but it's a challenging prop that develops stability and coordination. Build up to the Double-Leg Stretch (#100) with crunches on the balance ball.

- Lie on a balance ball, with feet flat on the floor and hands clasped behind your head.
- Extend your legs to 45 degrees. Curl your head and neck, articulating your spine. Lower to the starting position.
- Perform slow and fluid movements for 10 repetitions.

105

Corkscrew

The Corkscrew develops your lateral flexion. This exercise involves rotating your legs in a circular motion while keeping your upper body and arms stable. The bigger and wider the circles, the tougher the workout. Try to keep your abdominals evenly engaged throughout the exercise.

rectus abdominis

obliquus internus*

iliopsoas*

pectineus*

sartorius

rectus femoris

Correct form
Keep your back and arms firmly pressed into the floor. Pull your shoulder blades down your back. If you feel any strain in your joints, bend your knees slightly.

Avoid
Don't hunch your shoulders or arch your back.

transversus abdominis*

soleus

gastrocnemius

semimembranosus

vastus lateralis

tensor fasciae latae

obliquus externus

- Lie on the floor with legs extended toward the ceiling. Press your legs and heels together and point your toes.
- Inhale, lowering your legs to the right. Continue circling, bringing your legs forward, then to your left, and back up to the center.
- Complete the circle on exhale. Perform 5 times in each direction.

Annotation Key
Bold text indicates target muscles
Black text indicates other working muscles
* indicates deep muscles

106
Hip Twist

Sit with your legs on the floor and arms behind your back. Inhale and lift your legs one at a time to 45 degrees. Exhale and lower your legs to your right. Circle your legs forward, to the left, and back to the front. Repeat 5 times in each direction.

107 Corkscrew on Roller

Lie with your hips on a foam roller. Keep your upper body on the floor and extend your arms out to the sides. Raise your legs to 90 degrees, hip-width apart, and point your toes. Slowly make small circles with your legs and repeat 5 times in each direction.

108 Pendulum

Lie on the floor with legs pointing toward the ceiling. Inhale and lower your legs to the right. Exhale and bring your legs back to the center. Inhale and lower your legs to the left and return to the starting position. Perform 5 sets.

109 Corkscrew with Ball

Lie on the floor with legs extended toward the ceiling and balance a medium Pilates ball between your ankles. Squeeze the ball with your legs and perform the exercise as in the Corkscrew (#105). Repeat 5 times in each direction.

110 Supported Corkscrew with Ball

Sit with your legs on the floor and prop yourself up on your forearms. Balance a medium Pilates ball between your ankles and squeeze. Perform the exercise as in the Corkscrew (#105). Repeat 5 times in each direction.

111 Advanced Corkscrew

Begin seated on the floor. Bring your legs and torso up to the Teaser V-shape, with your arms forward and parallel to the floor. Perform opposite circles with your arms and legs: Circle your arms upward and to the right while you circle your legs downward and to the left. Repeat 3 times in each direction.

112 Corkscrew with Magic Circle

Lie on the floor with legs extended toward the ceiling and balance a circle between your calves. Squeeze the circle with your legs and perform the exercise as in the Corkscrew (#105). Repeat 5 times in each direction.

113

Forward Lunge Stretch

The Forward Lunge boosts your muscle strength in your glutes and hamstrings and stretches your hip flexors. This functional exercise is very similar to the movement of everyday walking, so if you perform the stretch correctly, you will soon feel the benefits in your natural stride.

Annotation Key
Bold text indicates target muscles
Black text indicates other working muscles
* indicates deep muscles

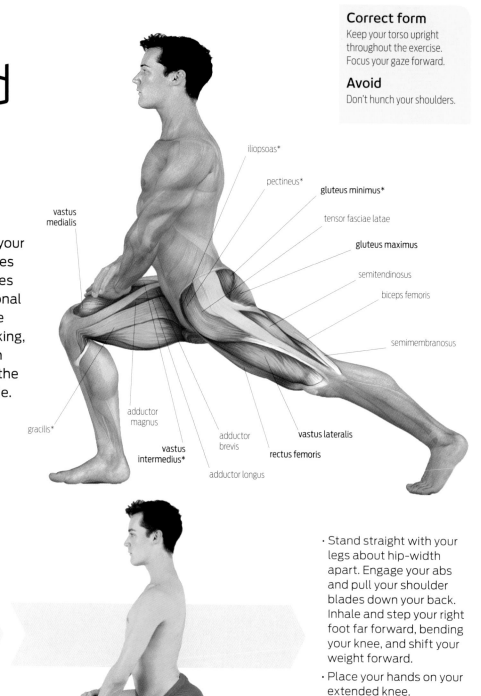

iliopsoas*
pectineus*
gluteus minimus*
tensor fasciae latae
gluteus maximus
semitendinosus
biceps femoris
semimembranosus
vastus medialis
gracilis*
adductor magnus
vastus intermedius*
adductor brevis
adductor longus
vastus lateralis
rectus femoris

- Stand straight with your legs about hip-width apart. Engage your abs and pull your shoulder blades down your back. Inhale and step your right foot far forward, bending your knee, and shift your weight forward.

- Place your hands on your extended knee.

- Return to standing position and repeat 5 times on each side.

114 Straight Lunge Stretch

The Straight Lunge Stretch focuses on stabilizing the hips and abs. Anchor your pelvis and lengthen your spine as you curl forward.

- Kneel on a mat and extend your right foot forward. Inhale and raise your arms overhead.
- Exhale and curl forward, bringing your chest toward your right thigh and touching your hands to the floor.
- Return to the starting position and repeat 5 times on each leg.

115 Bent Lunge Stretch 1

Kneel on a mat and extend your left foot forward. Inhale as you engage your abs and raise your arms overhead. Exhale and shift your weight forward while keeping your torso straight. Return to the starting position and repeat 5 times on each leg.

116 Bent Lunge Stretch 2

Kneel on a mat and extend your right foot forward. Inhale as you engage your abs and lengthen your spine. Exhale and shift your weight forward while keeping your torso straight. Bring your arms forward, parallel to the floor. Return to the starting position and repeat 5 times on each leg.

117 Bent Lunge Stretch 3

Kneel on a mat and extend your right foot forward. Inhale as you engage your abs and lengthen your spine. Clasp your hands behind you. Exhale and shift your weight forward while keeping your torso straight. Return to the starting position and repeat 5 times on each leg.

118

Side Lunge

The Side Lunge targets your inner and outer thighs as well as your glutes and quads. This exercise also stabilizes your core and helps improve your balance. As you progress, add light weights to your Side Lunge routine.

Annotation Key
Bold text indicates target muscles
Black text indicates other working muscles
* indicates deep muscles

Correct form
Tuck in your pelvis and control the movement. Keep your feet flat on the mat. Your knees should point in the same direction.

Avoid
Don't swing your hips out to the side.

deltoideus medialis

deltoideus anterior

obliquus externus

gluteus medius*

gluteus maximus

tensor fasciae latae

iliopsoas*

adductor longus

rectus femoris

vastus lateralis

vastus medialis

biceps femoris

gastrocnemius

soleus

transversus abdominis*

vastus intermedius*

adductor magnus

sartorius

gracilis*

- Stand upright with feet hip-width apart and arms at your sides. Inhale and engage your abs.
- Exhale, step your left foot out to the side, bending your knee. Extend your arms forward.
- Return to the standing position and repeat 5 times on each side.

119 Side Lunge with Arm Raises

Stand upright with your feet hip-width apart. Hold light weights at your sides. Inhale and engage your abs. Exhale and step your right foot out to the side, bending your knee, while raising your arms out to the sides. Return to the starting position and repeat 5 times.

120 Side Lunge Stretch

Stand upright with your feet hip-width apart and arms at your sides. Inhale and engage your abs. Exhale and step your left foot out to the side as you bend forward and touch the floor. Return to the standing position and repeat 5 times on each side.

121 Clock Lunge

Why perform only one type of lunge when you can do three at a time! The Clock Lunge combines the Forward, Side, and Reverse Lunges. Give your glutes a serious workout with this exercise.

- Stand upright with your feet hip-width apart and hands on your hips. Inhale and engage your abs.
- Exhale, step your right foot into a forward lunge, and return to center.
- Step your right foot into a side lunge and return to the front. Step your right foot back in a backward lunge.
- Continue moving clockwise for 5 repetitions.

122

Bridge

The Bridge tones your glutes and legs without putting pressure on your joints or lower back. The Bridge is a great exercise to improve spinal alignment and flexibility as you slowly and deliberately articulate the spine. It benefits your overall balance too.

Correct form
Place your feet close to your hips. Create a straight line from your shoulders to your knees and keep your hips level.

Avoid
Don't lift your hips too high and avoid arching your back.

Annotation Key
Bold text indicates target muscles
Black text indicates other working muscles
* indicates deep muscles

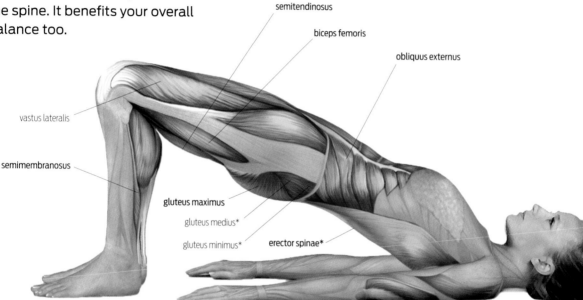

rectus abdominis
obliquus internus*
transversus abdominis*
iliopsoas*
pectineus*
sartorius
vastus intermedius*
rectus femoris
vastus medialis

semitendinosus
biceps femoris
obliquus externus
vastus lateralis
semimembranosus
gluteus maximus
gluteus medius*
gluteus minimus*
erector spinae*

- Lie on the floor with knees bent and feet close to your hips. Place your arms at your sides and inhale.
- On an exhale, curl your tailbone and your back, one vertebra at a time, from the mat.
- Hold the Bridge for a breath.
- Curl your spine slowly back down to the mat. Repeat 10 times.

123 Bridging Leg Lifts

Lie on your back with knees bent and arms at your sides. Inhale and lift your right leg into tabletop position. Exhale and curl your back off the mat. Hold the Bridge for a breath. Curl your spine back down to the mat. Repeat 5 times per leg.

124 Tabletop Bridge with Ball

Lie on your back with your arms at your sides. Balance a medium Pilates ball between your knees and lift your legs into tabletop. Exhale, curl your back from the floor, and squeeze the ball. Hold for a breath. Curl your spine down to the floor and repeat 5 times.

125 Piriformis Bridge

Lie on your back with knees bent and arms at your sides. Inhale and cross your left ankle over your right knee. Exhale as you curl your back from the mat. Hold the Bridge for a breath. Curl your spine slowly back down to the mat. Repeat 5 times on each leg.

126 Roller Bridge Pull-In

Lie on your back with knees bent. Rest your feet on a foam roller and inhale. Exhale as you curl your spine from the mat. Hold for a breath. Curl your spine back down to the mat. Repeat 5 times.

127 Bridge Gluteal Lift

Lie on your back with knees bent and arms at your sides. Inhale and lift your right leg straight up toward the ceiling. Exhale and curl your back from the mat, keeping your right leg extended. Hold the Bridge for a breath. Curl your spine back down to the mat. Repeat 5 times per leg.

128

Tabletop March

Building on the basic Bridge (#122),
the Tabletop March requires you
to hold the Bridge position while
incorporating leg lifts
and lowers.

Correct form
Try to keep your hips stable
and aligned throughout the
exercise. Keep a straight
line from your shoulders to
your knees.

Avoid
Don't drop your hips or pelvis
as you raise and lower
your legs.

Annotation Key
Bold text indicates target muscles
Black text indicates other working muscles
* indicates deep muscles

vastus medialis
adductor longus
sartorius
adductor brevis
obliquus internus*
transversus abdominis*
pectineus*
rectus abdominis
obliquus externus
adductor magnus
vastus intermedius*
rectus femoris
vastus lateralis
biceps femoris
iliopsoas*
gluteus maximus
gluteus medius*

- Lie on your back with
  knees bent and arms at
  your sides.

- Exhale and curl your back
  off the mat, one vertebra
  at a time. Inhale and lift
  your left leg into tabletop
  position, flexing your foot.
  Lower your foot.

- Repeat on your right
  leg and "march" for 5
  repetitions on each leg.

129 Bridge and Thigh Press with Ball

Lie on your back with knees bent and arms at your sides. Place a medium Pilates ball between your knees and inhale. Curl your back off the mat and squeeze the ball. Hold for 20 seconds, lower, and repeat 5 times.

130 Bridge with Leg Lifts

Begin in Bridge position. Inhale and extend your right leg to 45 degrees, pointing your toes. Lower your leg until parallel to the floor and flex your foot. Raise your leg back to 45 degrees. Repeat 5 times on each leg.

131 Bridge with Circle

Lie on your back with knees bent and arms at your sides. Place a magic circle between your thighs and inhale. Curl your back off the mat and squeeze the circle. Hold for 20 seconds, lower, and repeat 5 times.

132 Bridge Leg Drop

Begin in Bridge (#122) position. Inhale and extend your right leg toward the ceiling, pointing your toes. Lower your leg to 45 degrees and extend your leg back upward. Repeat 5 times on each leg.

133 Bridge on Swiss Ball

Sit on a Swiss ball with legs hip-width apart. Inhale and extend your arms in front of you. Exhale as you walk your feet out and curl your spine onto the ball. Raise your arms toward the ceiling and hold for 20 seconds. Curl up slowly to the starting position.

134

Low Plank

The Low Plank builds a strong foundation for other plank positions. It strengthens your entire body and enhances spinal stability. Control your breathing and concentrate on maintaining proper form. Build up to holding the position for 60 seconds.

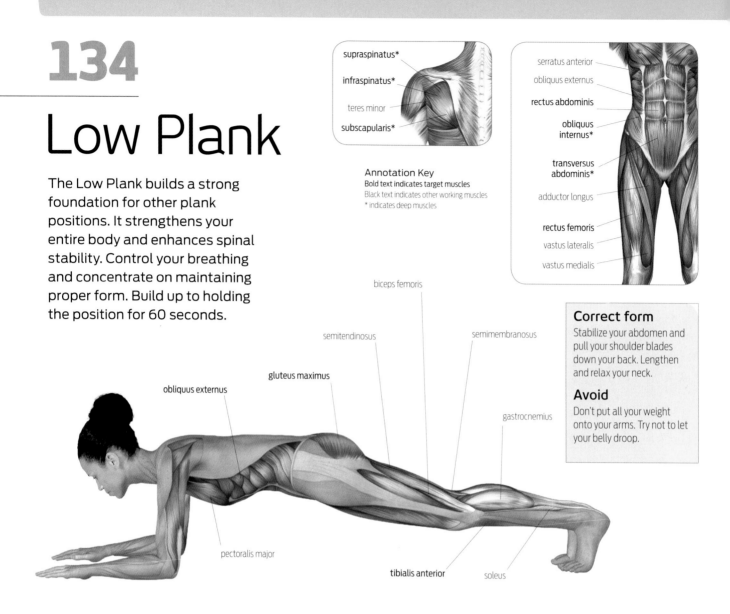

supraspinatus*
infraspinatus*
teres minor
subscapularis*

serratus anterior
obliquus externus
rectus abdominis
obliquus internus*
transversus abdominis*
adductor longus
rectus femoris
vastus lateralis
vastus medialis

Annotation Key
Bold text indicates target muscles
Black text indicates other working muscles
* indicates deep muscles

biceps femoris

semitendinosus

semimembranosus

gluteus maximus

obliquus externus

gastrocnemius

pectoralis major

tibialis anterior

soleus

Correct form
Stabilize your abdomen and pull your shoulder blades down your back. Lengthen and relax your neck.

Avoid
Don't put all your weight onto your arms. Try not to let your belly droop.

- Lie facedown on a mat with your arms extended overhead and toes pointed.
- Push your body up and rest your forearms on the floor, forming a straight line from your shoulders to your feet.
- Hold for several breaths, lower to the mat, and repeat 5 times.

135 Forearm Plank Knee Drops

Assume the Low Plank position (#134). Keeping your torso stable and your hips level, bend your left leg and touch your knee to the mat. Slowly return to Low Plank and alternate legs for 5 sets on each leg.

136 Spiderman Plank

Begin in the Low Plank (#134). Keep your torso stable and your hips level as you bend your left leg and lift it out to the side, reaching your knee toward your elbow. Hold for a few breaths. Alternate legs for 5 sets on each leg.

137 Arm Reach Plank

Assume the Low Plank position (#134). Keeping your torso stable and your hips level, extend your right arm to the side, parallel to the floor. Slowly return to Low Plank and alternate arms for 5 sets on each arm.

138 Low-to-High Plank

Begin in the Low Plank position (#134). Straighten your right arm, then your left arm to assume the High Plank position (#156). Hold for a few breaths. Lower your left arm, followed by your right arm. Hold and repeat 5 times.

139 Plank with Leg and Arm Lifts

This Plank teaches you how to balance while using oppositional forces. Feel the energy release from your hands and toes as you lift and pull your limbs in opposite directions.

- Assume the Low Plank position (#134). Stabilize your torso and lengthen your neck as you inhale.
- Extend your left arm straight forward while lifting your right leg behind you to about hip height.
- Hold for a breath, lower, and alternate sides for a total of 10 repetitions.

140

Side-Lying Leg Kicks

The Side-Lying Leg Kicks increase mobility in your hip joints and strengthen your thighs and abdominals. Focus on using your powerhouse muscles to stabilize your upper body during this movement. Engage your abs, pull your shoulder blades down your back, and move your legs in a precise and fluid movement.

Annotation Key
Bold text indicates target muscles
Black text indicates other working muscles
* indicates deep muscles

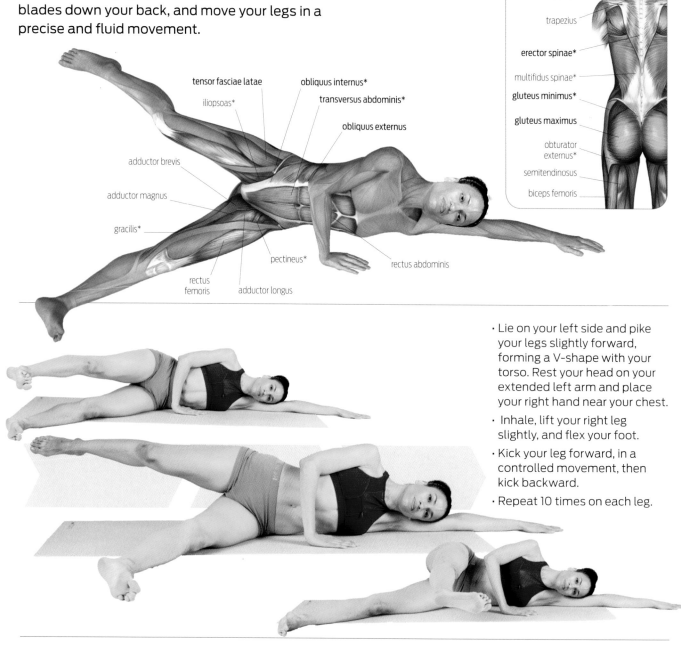

tensor fasciae latae
iliopsoas*
obliquus internus*
transversus abdominis*
obliquus externus
adductor brevis
adductor magnus
gracilis*
pectineus*
rectus abdominis
rectus femoris
adductor longus

semispinalis*
levator scapulae*
trapezius
erector spinae*
multifidus spinae*
gluteus minimus*
gluteus maximus
obturator externus*
semitendinosus
biceps femoris

- Lie on your left side and pike your legs slightly forward, forming a V-shape with your torso. Rest your head on your extended left arm and place your right hand near your chest.
- Inhale, lift your right leg slightly, and flex your foot.
- Kick your leg forward, in a controlled movement, then kick backward.
- Repeat 10 times on each leg.

141 Side-Lying Leg Sweeps
Lie on your left side and pike your legs slightly forward. Rest your head on your left hand and place your right hand near your chest. Perform the exercise as in Side-Lying Leg Kicks (#140). Repeat 10 times on each side.

142 Side-Lying Bicycle Sweeps
Lie on your left side and pike your legs slightly forward. Rest your head on your left hand and place your right hand near your chest. Inhale and lift your right leg to hip-height. Exhale, bend your right knee, and bring it forward in a controlled movement. Kick your leg backward and repeat 10 times on each side.

143 Advanced Side Kick

Keep your torso off the floor in the Advanced Side Kick to increase the level of difficulty in this exercise series.

- Lie on your right side and pike your legs slightly forward, forming a V-shape with your torso.
- Rise up on your right elbow and clasp your hands behind your head.
- Inhale, lift your left leg slightly, and flex your foot.
- Kick your leg forward, in a controlled movement, then kick backward. Repeat 10 times on each side.

144 Side-Lying Ankle Press with Circle

Lie on your right side and pike your legs forward, forming a V-shape with your body. Rest your head on your right hand. Place a magic circle between your ankles and press your left leg down toward the floor. Hold for 20 seconds and repeat on the other side.

145 Side-Kneeling Leg Lifts

From a kneeling position, extend your right leg out to the side. Lean to the left and place your left hand on the floor at your side. Place your right hand on your hip. Stabilize your torso as you lift your right leg to the side. Hold for 10 seconds and lower. Repeat 5 times on each side.

146 Side-Kneeling Leg Circles

From a kneeling position, extend your left leg to the side and place your right hand on the floor at your side. Place your left hand on your hip. Stabilize your torso as you lift your left leg to the side. Circle your leg forward, down, and back. Return to the starting position and repeat 5 times on each side.

147 Side-Kneeling Leg Sweeps

The Side-Kneeling Leg Sweeps help improve your balance and increase the flexibility in your hip flexors. This exercise also challenges your core.

- Kneel on the floor and extend your right leg to the side. Lean onto your left hand and inhale.
- Lift your right leg off the floor to just below hip height.
- Exhale and swing your leg forward and back, keeping your pelvis stable. Repeat 5 times on each side.

148

Low Side Plank

The Low Side Plank improves your balance and posture and builds up your stamina. It is also an excellent workout for your obliques, hips, and upper arms. Be conscious of keeping your whole body in proper alignment and move with controlled precision.

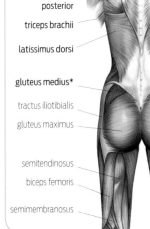

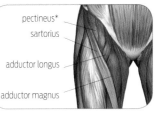

serratus anterior

rectus abdominis

transversus abdominis*

tensor fasciae latae

rectus femoris

vastus lateralis

tibialis anterior

deltoideus anterior

obliquus externus

obliquus internus*

biceps brachii

brachialis

soleus

Annotation Key
Bold text indicates target muscles
Black text indicates other working muscles
* indicates deep muscles

Correct form
Pull your hips and shoulders upward and lengthen your neck. Press your sit bones together to help stabilize your pelvis.

Avoid
Don't hunch your shoulders or drop your hips.

- Begin in a Low Plank position (#134) with your feet about hip-width apart and elbows directly beneath your shoulders. Inhale and pull your navel into your spine.

- Exhale, rotate your body to the right, and reach your right arm toward the ceiling.

- Hold for several breaths and return to the starting position. Repeat 3 times per side.

149 Side-Kneeling Leg Raises

Begin in a kneeling position. Extend your right leg out to the side and lean to the left. Place your left hand on the floor at your side and extend your right arm overhead. As you lift your right leg, lower your right arm to meet your leg. Repeat 5 times per side.

150 Side Bend

Lie on your left side with your head on your left arm. Place your right hand on the floor in front of you. Move your top ankle slightly in front of the other. Bring your left hand in near your shoulder and straighten your left arm as you lift up from the floor. Reach your right arm overhead. Repeat 3 times per side.

151 High Side Plank on Hand

The High Side Plank on Hand stabilizes your hips, torso, and shoulders while strengthening your core and arm muscles.

- Kneel on a mat and assume a High Plank position (#156). Rotate your torso up and to the right, extending your right arm toward the ceiling.
- Gaze upward and pull your hips and arm upward.
- Hold for 20 seconds, release, and repeat 3 times per side.

152 Side Bend with Twist

Sit on your right hip and lean on your right arm. Place your left hand on the floor in front of you and rest your left ankle slightly in front of your right foot. Inhale, lift your body, and extend your left arm overhead. Exhale and reach your left hand under your chest. Repeat 3 times on each side.

153 Star Hold

Sit on your left hip and lean on your left hand. Place your right hand on the floor in front of you. Lift your body from the floor. Extend your right arm overhead and raise your right leg to hip level. Hold for 10 seconds, lower, and repeat 5 times on each side.

154 Star with Arm and Leg Lowers

Sit on your left hip and lean on your left hand. Place your right hand on the floor in front of you. Lift your body from the floor. Extend your right arm overhead and lift your right leg to hip level. Lower your arm and leg, lift them back up, and repeat 5 times on each side.

155 Side-Kneeling Leg Kicks Advanced

Stability, strength, and balance all come into play in this challenging Leg Kick variation.

- From a kneeling position, extend your left leg out to the side.
- Lean to the right, clasping your hands behind your head.
- Engage your abs and keep your torso stable as you lift and lower your left leg to the side.
- Repeat 5 times per leg.

High Plank

The High Plank offers a full-body workout, strengthening your core, shoulders, arms, legs, and glutes. Because it integrates the whole body, you need to actively coordinate all your mobilization muscles for this exercise. Work up to holding the High Plank for 60 seconds.

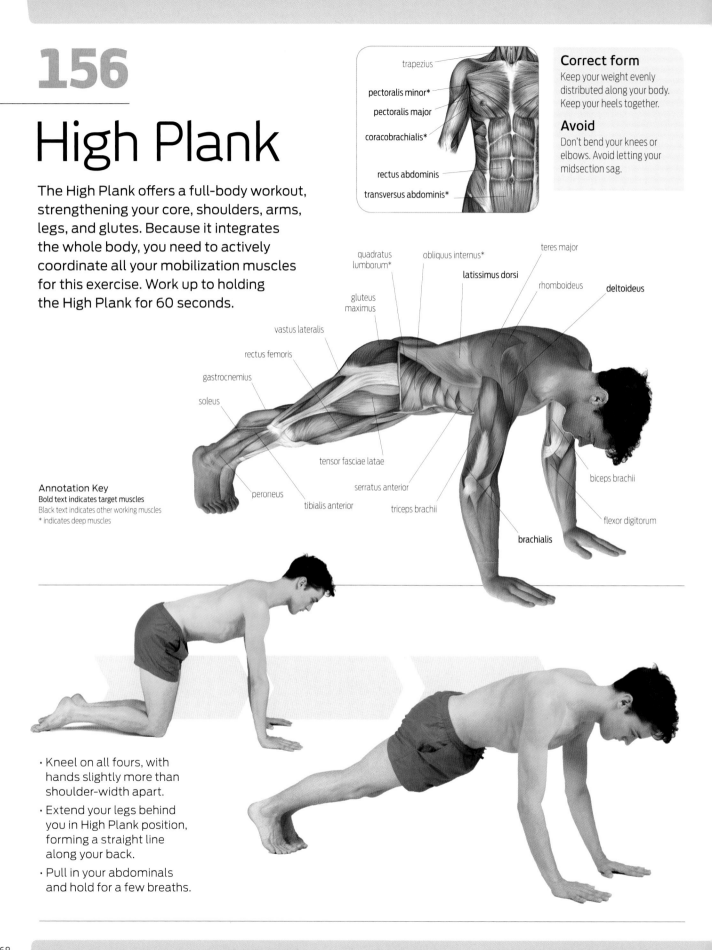

Correct form
Keep your weight evenly distributed along your body. Keep your heels together.

Avoid
Don't bend your knees or elbows. Avoid letting your midsection sag.

trapezius
pectoralis minor*
pectoralis major
coracobrachialis*
rectus abdominis
transversus abdominis*

quadratus lumborum*
obliquus internus*
teres major
latissimus dorsi
rhomboideus
deltoideus
gluteus maximus
vastus lateralis
rectus femoris
gastrocnemius
soleus
tensor fasciae latae
serratus anterior
biceps brachii
peroneus
tibialis anterior
triceps brachii
flexor digitorum
brachialis

Annotation Key
Bold text indicates target muscles
Black text indicates other working muscles
* indicates deep muscles

- Kneel on all fours, with hands slightly more than shoulder-width apart.
- Extend your legs behind you in High Plank position, forming a straight line along your back.
- Pull in your abdominals and hold for a few breaths.

157 Leg Pull Front

Assume the High Plank position (#156) with feet about hip-width apart and inhale. On exhale, lift your right leg to hip height, foot flexed. Inhale and lower your leg. Alternate legs for 5 sets.

158 Leg Pull Extensions

Begin in the High Plank position (#156) with feet about hip-width apart and inhale. On exhale, lift your right leg and left arm. Inhale and lower. Alternate opposite arms and legs for 10 sets.

159 High Plank Knee Pull-In

Assume the High Plank position (#156) with feet hip-width apart and inhale. On exhale, bring your left knee in toward your chest and curl your head down. Inhale and return to the starting position. Perform 5 times on each leg.

160 High Plank with Knee Twist

Assume the High Plank position (#156) with feet about hip-width apart and inhale. On exhale, bring your right knee in toward your chest and twist it to your left as you curl your head down. Inhale and return to the starting position. Repeat 5 times on each leg.

161 Monkey Walk

Stand straight. Bend from the waist and reach your hands to the floor. Walk your hands and feet apart until you reach High Plank position. Form a straight line along your back, from shoulders to heels. Pull in your abdominals and hold for a few breaths.

162

High Plank Pike

The Plank Pike is a rejuvenating inversion exercise that improves circulation and reduces neck tension. The Plank Pike lengthens the spine by opening up the space between the individual vertebrae, alleviating spinal compression. And like all planks, it's an excellent full-body workout.

iliopsoas*

erector spinae*

biceps femoris

semitendinosus

semimembranosus

gastrocnemius

latissimus dorsi

serratus anterior

trapezius

deltoideus posterior

transversus abdominis

soleus

biceps brachii

rectus abdominis

rectus femoris

tibialis anterior

triceps brachii

- Assume a High Plank position (#156) with feet hip-width apart.

- Lift your hips, forming an inverted V-position. Push your heels into the floor and hold for a few breaths.

- Pivot your shoulders and hips into High Plank. Hold for a few breaths and repeat 5 times.

163 Pike on Roller

Begin in the High Plank position (#156) with a foam roller under your shins. Pivot your hips and shoulders, lifting your hips high, and hold for a few breaths. Slowly lower back into High Plank. Repeat 5 times.

164 Pike on Swiss Ball

Begin in the High Plank position (#156) with a Swiss ball positioned under your shins. Pivot your hips and shoulders, lifting your hips high, and hold for a few breaths. Slowly lower into High Plank. Repeat 5 times.

165 Plank Knee Pull-In

The Plank Knee Pull-In improves your coordination and balance. You'll also build core strength and gain flexibility in your hamstrings and calves.

· Assume the High Plank position (#156). Pull your left knee into your chest.

· Extend your left leg up toward the ceiling, forming a straight line from your hands to your raised leg.

· Hold for a few breaths and alternate sides for 3 sets on each leg.

Reverse Plank

The Reverse Plank enhances shoulder stability and builds arm and core strength. It also engages your lower back, deltoids, and glutes. If your shoulders are not quite flexible enough to perform this exercise, modify on your forearms first and build your way up to the full Reverse Plank.

Annotation Key
Bold text indicates target muscles
Black text indicates other working muscles
* indicates deep muscles

Correct form
Open your chest and form a long, straight line from your shoulders to your heels. If your shoulders or chest are uncomfortable, slightly alter your hand position.

Avoid
Try not to drop your hips or tense your neck.

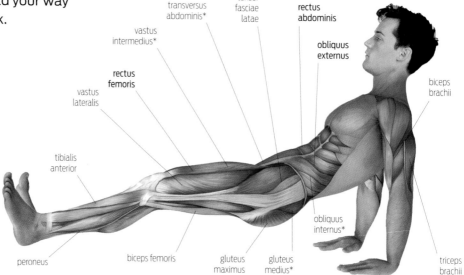

* Sit with legs forward and hands behind you, fingers facing your hips.
* Push into your hands and lift your chest and hips.
* Keeping your pelvis stable, hold for several breaths, and slowly lower.

167 Reverse Plank Leg Pull

Begin in the Reverse Plank position (#166). Keeping your hips aligned and pelvis stable, lift your right leg. Flex your foot, hold for a breath, and lower. Alternate legs and repeat 5 times on each leg.

168 Front Plank March

Sit on the floor with knees bent and hands behind your back. Lift up your hips so your torso is parallel to the floor. Lift your left leg to tabletop, hold for a breath, and lower. Perform 10 repetitions on each leg.

169 Triceps Dip

The Triceps Dip targets your upper arms and, like the Reverse Plank, improves flexibility in your shoulder joints. Try to balance on your heels for maximum benefit from this powerhouse exercise.

- Sit on the floor with knees bent. Place your arms behind you, with bent elbows and fingers pointing forward.
- Straighten your arms and lift your hips from the mat.
- Push down into your heels and lift your toes from the mat.
- Slowly lower your torso almost to the mat and lift up for 5 dips.

170

Teaser

The ultimate Pilates abdominal exercise, the Teaser challenges your balance and your core. The Teaser takes some practice to accomplish, but your efforts will be rewarded with a stronger powerhouse and improved spinal stability.

Annotation Key
Bold text indicates target muscles
Black text indicates other working muscles
* indicates deep muscles

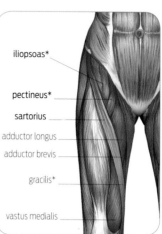

iliopsoas*
pectineus*
sartorius
adductor longus
adductor brevis
gracilis*
vastus medialis

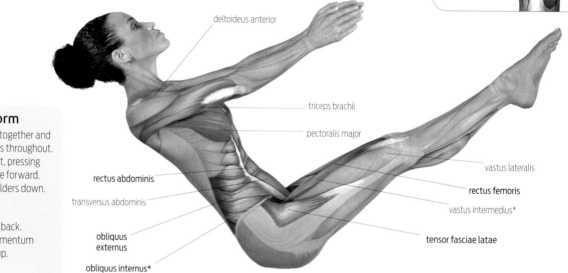

deltoideus anterior

triceps brachii

pectoralis major

rectus abdominis

transversus abdominis

vastus lateralis

rectus femoris

vastus intermedius*

tensor fasciae latae

obliquus externs

obliquus internus*

Correct form
Press your legs together and engage your abs throughout. Open your chest, pressing your breastbone forward. Keep your shoulders down.

Avoid
Don't arch your back. Avoid using momentum to lift yourself up.

- Lie on your back with arms overhead. Pull in your abs and inhale.
- On exhale, curl your torso up while lifting your legs, forming a V-shape with your torso and legs.
- Raise your arms parallel to your legs.
- Slowly lower and repeat 3 times.

171 Teaser Prep

Sit with knees bent and arms overhead. Pull in your abs and inhale. Articulate your spine as you roll onto your lower back and extend your arms parallel to the floor. Hold for a few breaths and repeat 3 times.

172 One-Leg Teaser

Lie on your back with knees bent and arms overhead. Pull in your abs and inhale. Curl your torso off the mat to 45 degrees, articulating your spine. Raise your right leg to 45 degrees and hold for several breaths. Keep your arms parallel to the floor. Slowly lower and repeat 5 times.

173 Teaser Modified

Lie on your back with knees bent and arms overhead. Pull in your abs and inhale. Curl your torso off the mat to 45 degrees, articulating your spine, as you lift your legs to 45 degrees. Extend your arms to shoulder height and hold for several breaths. Lower and repeat 5 times.

174 Teaser Stacking Spine

Lie on your back with knees bent and arms overhead. Inhale and articulate your spine off the mat. Reach your arms overhead and hold the stacked spine for a breath. Lift your legs to 45 degrees, forming a V-shape with your torso and legs. Lower and repeat 5 times.

175 Teaser on Swiss Ball

The Swiss ball adds support for your legs but demands precise control over your balance. This Teaser will improve your spinal alignment and strengthen your core.

- Lie on your back and position your calves on a Swiss ball. Inhale and engage your abs.
- Slowly peel your spine from the mat and exhale. Keep a slight C-curve in your lower back and extend your arms forward.
- Hold for a few breaths, lower, and repeat 5 times.

176 Teaser Frog Legs

Lie on your back with knees bent and arms overhead. Curl your torso to 45 degrees, press your heels together, and slightly open your knees. Lift your feet off the floor. Exhale and extend your legs to 45 degrees, keeping your feet flexed. Lower and repeat 3 times.

177 Teaser Frog Legs Twist

Prepare as in Teaser Frog Legs (#176), except on the leg extension, point your toes and twist to your right, opening your arms wide. Lower and repeat 3 times on each side.

178

Side-Lying Double-Leg Lift

In the Side-Lying Double-Leg Lift, you need to lift both legs at the same time. Squeeze your legs together to engage your thighs and glutes. This exercise targets the obliques and improves the range of motion in your hips.

Correct form
Keep your spine neutral and lengthen your torso. Stack your legs, shoulders, and hips for stability.

Avoid
Don't roll your hips to assist with the movement. Avoid relying on your hand to push your legs up.

Annotation Key
Bold text indicates target muscles
Black text indicates other working muscles
* indicates deep muscles

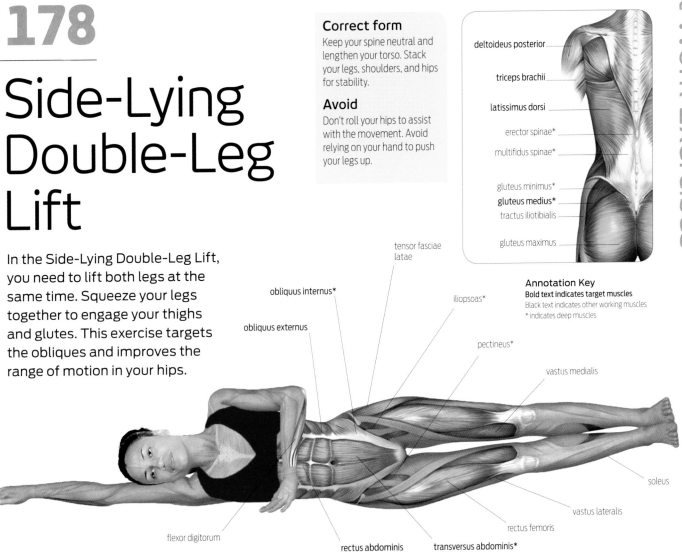

deltoideus posterior
triceps brachii
latissimus dorsi
erector spinae*
multifidus spinae*
gluteus minimus*
gluteus medius*
tractus iliotibialis
gluteus maximus

tensor fasciae latae
obliquus internus*
obliquus externus
iliopsoas*
pectineus*
vastus medialis
soleus
vastus lateralis
rectus femoris
flexor digitorum
rectus abdominis
transversus abdominis*

- Lie on your side, with your head resting on your extended right arm. Place your left hand on the floor.
- Press your legs together and lift them, stretching them from the hip sockets.
- Lower and repeat 3 times on each side.

179 Side-Lying Double-Leg Lift with Ball

Lie on your side with a Pilates ball between your ankles. Rest your head on your extended left arm and place your right hand on the floor. Squeeze the ball, lift your legs, and hold for a breath. Lower and repeat 3 times on each leg.

180 Side-Lying Double-Leg Lift on Roller

Lie on your left side with a foam roller under your hips. Place your left forearm on the floor, and your right hand on your hip. Squeeze your legs together, lift, and hold for a few breaths. Lower and repeat 3 times on each side.

181 Side-Lying Arch-Up

Lie on your left side, resting your head on your extended left arm. Place your right hand on the floor in front of you. Squeeze your legs together. Lift your legs and raise your torso from the mat. Hold for a few breaths and lower. Repeat 3 times on each side.

182 Side-Lying Scissors

Lie on your side, propped up on your left elbow. Lift your legs a few inches from the floor. Alternate moving your legs forward and backward in a scissors motion. Lower and repeat 3 times on each side.

183 Side-Lying Bicycle

Lie on your side, propped up on your left elbow. Bend your right knee forward, straighten your leg, then swing your leg behind you. Bend your knee and repeat 5 times on each side.

184 Clam

Lie on your side, propped up on your left elbow. Bend your knees behind you and lift your feet from the floor. Keeping your feet together, lift your right knee into Clam position, and hold for a breath. Lower and repeat 3 times on each side.

185 Clam Leg Extension

Lie on your side, propped up on your left elbow. Bend your knees behind you and lift your feet from the floor. Keeping your feet together, lift your right knee into Clam position. Extend your right leg straight up, return your right leg to the Clam position, and repeat 3 times. Lower and repeat on the other leg.

186 Side-Lying Lower-Leg Lift

Lie on your side, propped up on your right elbow. Place your left hand on the floor. Lift your left leg to about shoulder height. Raise your right leg to meet the left, lower your right leg almost to the mat, and repeat 3 times on each side.

187

Side Leg Series

The Side Leg Series challenges your stamina and coordination with leg pulses and subtle shifts of leg position. As with other leg lifts, this exercise also engages your core muscles, thighs, and glutes. To protect your lower back from straining, position yourself at a slight pike through your hips, forming a V-shape with your torso and legs.

Correct form
Stack your shoulders and hips. Engage your abs and keep your torso stable. Slightly rotate your raised foot down toward the mat.

Avoid
Don't rock your torso or shift your hips.

erector spinae

quadratus lumborum*
gluteus minimus*
gluteus medius*

gluteus maximus

semitendinosus

biceps femoris

semimembranosus

tensor fasciae latae

iliopsoas*

pectineus*

obliquus externus

rectus abdominis

rectus femoris

adductor longus

gracilis*

obliquus internus*

transversus abdominis*

vastus intermedius*

sartorius

- Lie on your right side, resting your head on your right arm.
- Flex your feet. Lift your left leg a few inches off the floor and lower, pulsing up and down 5 times.
- Point your left toes and pulse 5 times.
- Next, lift your left leg above hip height. Pulse 5 times with your foot flexed, and 5 times with pointed toes.
- Alternate sides and repeat.

188 Leg Lift Supported

Lie on your right side, propped up on your elbow, and stack your legs. Lift your left leg to hip height, lower, and pulse up and down 5 times. Next, lift your left to 45 degrees and lower for 5 more pulses. Alternate sides and repeat.

189 Side Leg Circles

Lie on your left side, propped up on your elbow. Bend your left knee and point your toes. Lift your right leg to hip height and circle your leg clockwise 5 times, then counterclockwise 5 times. Alternate sides and repeat.

190 Hot Potato Leg Taps

Lie on your right side, propped up on your elbow. Lift your left leg and tap your toes in front of your right foot then behind for 10 repetitions. Alternate sides and repeat.

191 Inner-Thigh Lift

Lie on your right side, propped up on your elbow. Place your left foot in front of your right hip and hold your ankle with your left hand. Point your right toes and pulse your right leg 10 times. Alternate sides and repeat.

192 Inner-Thigh Lift with Ball

Lie on your right side, resting your head on your extended arm. Support your left knee on a Pilates ball. Place your left hand in front of your chest. Point your toes and pulse your lower leg 10 times. Repeat on the other side.

193

Waistline Warrior

The Waistline Warrior targets the obliques and is an excellent exercise for a sleeker abdomen. The spinal rotation of this exercise improves the definition in your waistline without adding too much bulk. If you need extra support for your lower back, place a medium ball behind you.

Annotation Key
Bold text indicates target muscles
Black text indicates other working muscles
* indicates deep muscles

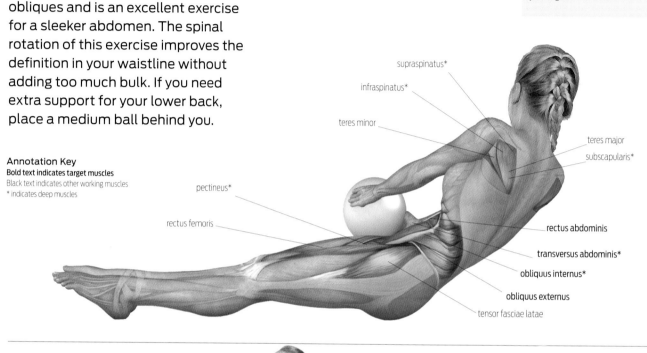

supraspinatus*

infraspinatus*

teres minor

teres major

subscapularis*

pectineus*

rectus femoris

rectus abdominis

transversus abdominis*

obliquus internus*

obliquus externus

tensor fasciae latae

- Sit on the floor with legs forward and toes pointed. Hold a weighted ball in front of you and inhale.
- Curl your lower back slightly and exhale.
- Slowly twist your torso and arms to the right, return to center, and twist to the left.
- Repeat 10 times to each side.

194 Figure 8

The Figure 8 adds an extra dimension to the Waistline Warrior exercise. This exercise has you making Figure 8s with your arms as you twist and flex your obliques.

- Sit with legs forward, holding a small weighted ball in front of you. Curl your lower back slightly.
- Slowly twist to the right and circle your arms down and to the right, then up and around to center.
- Twist to the left and down, then up and back to center. Repeat 5 times in each direction.

195 C-Curve Arm Cross

Sit with your legs forward and toes pointed. Support your lower back on a medium ball and hold small weights in either hand in front of you. Curl your lower back slightly. Cross your right wrist over the left, then your left wrist over the right, for 10 repetitions.

196 Hula

Sit with knees bent and curl your lower back slightly. Extend your hands parallel to the floor and lift your feet off the mat. Slowly twist your torso and arms to the left while twisting your knees to the right. Return to center and twist to the opposite side. Repeat 10 times to each side.

197 Hula with Ball

Sit with knees bent and curl your lower back slightly. Holding a small weighted ball, extend your hands parallel to the floor, and lift your feet off the mat. Slowly twist your torso and arms to the right and twist your knees to the left. Return to center, and twist to the opposite side. Repeat 10 times to each side.

198

Push-Up

Similar to the High Plank, the time-tested Push-Up is a great addition to any Pilates routine. The Push-Up touches on key aspects of Pilates: controlled movement, precise form, and deliberate breathing. This exercise benefits not only your chest muscles and shoulder joints but also your arms, core, and legs.

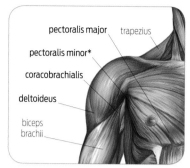

pectoralis major
trapezius
pectoralis minor*
coracobrachialis
deltoideus
biceps brachii

Correct form
Form a straight line with your body, from your shoulders to your heels. Lengthen your spine and gaze downward.

Avoid
Don't lift up your hips or strain your neck.

Annotation Key
Bold text indicates target muscles
Black text indicates other working muscles
* indicates deep muscles

quadratus lumborum*
obliquus internus*
obliquus externus
vastus intermedius*
gluteus maximus
serratus anterior
vastus medialis
rectus abdominis
vastus lateralis
transversus abdominis*
rectus femoris
iliopsoas*

- From standing position, lower your hands to the floor, shoulder-width apart. Extend your legs behind you, legs pressed together. Your wrists should be in line with your shoulders.

- Engage your abs and inhale. Bend your elbows, and exhale as you lower your chest toward the floor.

- Inhale and lift up. Perform 10 repetitions.

199 Push-Up on Knees
Kneel on your hands and knees. Lift your feet off the floor behind you and perform the exercise as in the Push-Up (#198). Repeat 15 times.

200 Push-Up on Roller
Kneel on the floor and place your hands shoulder-width apart on a foam roller. Extend your legs behind you. Perform the exercise as in the Push-Up (#198) for 10 repetitions.

201 Triceps Push-Up
Kneel on your hands and knees. Extend your legs behind you. Place your hands on the mat slightly less than shoulder-width apart. Engage your abs and inhale. Exhale as you lower your chest toward the floor. Inhale and lift up. Perform 10 repetitions.

202 Push-Up with Roller Switch
Assume a Push-Up position with a foam roller placed parallel to your body and under your right shoulder. Lower your chest and lift up for 1 Push-Up, and push the roller to your left. Place your left hand on the roller and perform another Push-Up. Repeat the series in reverse for a total of 20 Push-Ups.

203 Push-Up on Balance Ball
Kneel on the floor and place your hands shoulder-width apart on a balance ball. Extend your legs behind you. Perform the exercise as in the Push-Up (#198) for 10 repetitions.

204

Heel Beats

Few Pilates moves firm up the glutes as well as Heel Beats. You'll also strengthen your lower back, hamstrings, and inner thighs. The quick tapping motion requires a bit of focus: You need to keep your abdominals engaged and your breathing at a steady rhythm.

Annotation Key
Bold text indicates target muscles
Black text indicates other working muscles
* indicates deep muscles

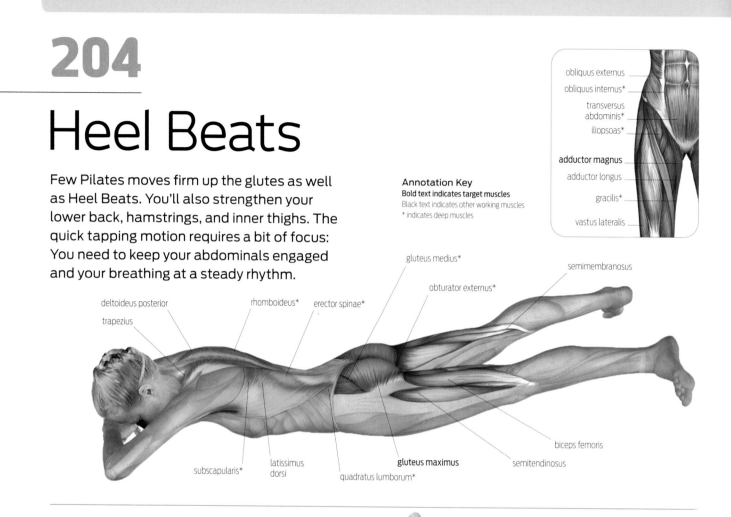

obliquus externus
obliquus internus*
transversus abdominis*
iliopsoas*
adductor magnus
adductor longus
gracilis*
vastus lateralis

gluteus medius*
obturator externus*
semimembranosus
deltoideus posterior
rhomboideus*
erector spinae*
trapezius
subscapularis*
latissimus dorsi
quadratus lumborum*
gluteus maximus
semitendinosus
biceps femoris

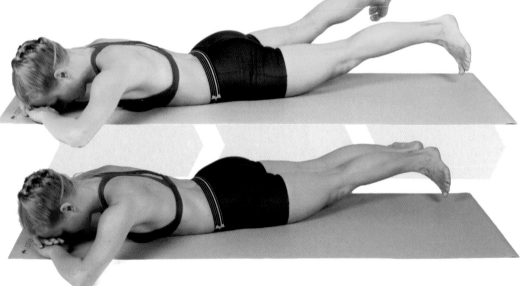

Correct form
Pull your shoulder blades down your back. Keep your feet flexed and slightly turned out throughout. Place a towel under your hips for support if needed.

Avoid
Don't raise your legs too high.

- Lie facedown with legs extended and feet flexed. Place your hands under your forehead.
- Inhale and press your heels and legs together.
- As you exhale, lift your legs, open your feet to hip width, then bring your legs together and tap your heels.
- Perform 5 heel beats for every exhale and inhale.

205 Double-Leg Kick Prone

Prone exercises such as the Double-Leg Kick Prone help strengthen the back and improve posture and mobility.

- Lie facedown with knees bent and toes pointed. Inhale and place your hands behind your back.
- Exhale, curl your head and upper chest from the mat, and swing your arm behind you at your sides; at the same time, lift your legs and extend your feet to hip width.
- Inhale, lower your legs, and repeat 10 times.

206 Leg Lift Prone with Circle

Lie facedown with a magic circle between your ankles. Rest your forehead on your hands and inhale. On exhale, squeeze the circle and hold for several breaths. Release and lower your legs. Perform 10 repetitions.

207 Swimming Seal

Lie facedown with legs extended and toes pointed. Place your hands under your forehead. Inhale and press your legs together. As you exhale, lift your legs and open your feet to hip width. Close your legs, tapping your feet together. Perform 5 taps for every exhale and inhale.

208 Facedown Snow Angel

Lie facedown with arms and legs extended and pressed together. Inhale to prepare. Exhale and lift your arms and legs, opening and closing them as if making snow angels. Repeat 5 times.

209

Single-Leg Heel Taps

Single-Leg Heel Taps enhance mobility in the hip flexors and lower back. Focus on engaging your transversus abdominis muscle, which wraps around your midsection like a corset. Move your legs with controlled precision, keeping your knees bent at 90 degrees.

Correct form
Your spine should be in a neutral position. Keep your torso stable throughout the exercise.

Avoid
Don't arch your back or force your lower back into the mat.

vastus medialis

sartorius

transversus abdominis*

rectus abdominis

obliquus internus*

obliquus externus

gluteus medius*

adductor magnus

vastus intermedius*

vastus lateralis

rectus femoris

iliopsoas*

gluteus maximus

- Lie on your back with arms flat at your sides. Lift your legs into tabletop position, feet flexed.
- Keeping your knees bent at 90 degrees, tap your left heel on the mat, while bringing your right knee in closer to your chest.
- Alternate legs for a total of 20 Heel Taps.

210 Double-Leg Heel Taps

Lie on your back with arms flat at your sides. Lift your legs into tabletop position, feet flexed, and inhale. Keeping your knees bent and feet together, exhale as you lower your legs and tap your heels on the mat. Return to tabletop and perform 20 repetitions.

211 Heel Taps with Ball

Lie on your back with arms flat at your sides. Place a small Pilates ball between your knees and inhale. Lift your legs into tabletop position and perform the exercise as in Double-Leg Heel Taps (#210). Repeat 20 times.

212 Frog

Lie on your back with arms flat at your sides. Lift your feet off the floor and press your heels together, dropping your knees to the sides. Keeping your heels together, exhale, and straighten your legs to 45 degrees. Perform 20 repetitions.

213 Frog with Band

Lie on your back and wrap a resistance band around your feet. Hold the ends in your hands and rest your elbows on the floor. Press your heels together and perform as in the Frog (#212). Repeat 20 times.

214 Frog Crunch with Band

Lie on your back. Wrap a resistance band around your feet and drop your knees to your sides. Hold the ends of the band and rest your elbows on the floor. Keeping your heels together, exhale as you straighten your legs to 45 degrees and curl your head and shoulders from the floor. Perform 20 repetitions.

215 Frog Press with Ball at Heels

Lie on your back with arms flat at your sides. Place a Pilates ball between your ankles and bring your knees into your chest, dropping your knees out to the sides. Straighten your legs and lower to Frog position for a total of 20 repetitions.

216

Child's Pose

The relaxing Child's Pose is the perfect stretch between more strenuous Pilates exercises. Focus on deep lateral breathing and feel your ribcage expand and contract along your thighs. As you elongate your spine and open the spaces between your vertebrae, feel the energy release through your arms and fingertips.

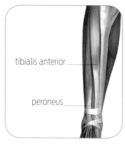

tibialis anterior

peroneus

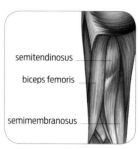

semitendinosus

biceps femoris

semimembranosus

Correct form
Form a C-curve in your back and open your shoulder blades. Relax your hips and your neck.

Avoid
Don't hunch your shoulders.

Annotation Key
Bold text indicates target muscles
Black text indicates other working muscles
* indicates deep muscles

latissimus dorsi

gluteus maximus

teres major

erector spinae*

trapezius

extensor digitorum

serratus anterior

- Kneel on the floor with knees hip-width apart. Lower your hips onto your heels.
- Inhale and extend your arms forward. Rest your forehead on the floor.
- Hold for several long, deep breaths.
- Exhale and curl up using your abs.

217 Child's Pose with Tucked Arms

Kneel on the floor with knees hip-width apart. Lower your hips onto your heels. Inhale and wrap your arms along your sides. Rest your forehead on the floor. Hold for several breaths. Exhale and curl up using your abs.

218 Child's Pose with Wide Knees

Kneel on the floor with your knees wider than hip-width apart and feet together. Lower your hips onto your heels and curl your torso forward, resting the side of your head on the mat. Inhale and drape your arms at your sides, pulling your shoulders away from your neck. Hold for several breaths. Exhale and curl up using your abs.

219 Child's Pose on Roller

If the Child's Pose (#216) strains your back, relieve some of the tension by resting your head higher up on a foam roller.

- Kneel on a mat with a foam roller under your chest and parallel to your body. Lower your hips onto your heels.
- Inhale, extend your arms forward, and rest your forehead on the roller. Hold for several deep breaths.
- Exhale and curl up using your abs.

220

Cat-to-Cow Stretch

The Cat-to-Cow Stretch activates the entire length of the spine, improving flexibility and relieving tension. Think of the oppositional forces of flexion (Cat) and extension (Cow) in this exercise. As you curl up your spine, envision pulling down from your head and tailbone. As you arch your back, pull upward through your neck and hips.

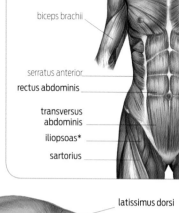

deltoideus anterior
biceps brachii
serratus anterior
rectus abdominis
transversus abdominis
iliopsoas*
sartorius

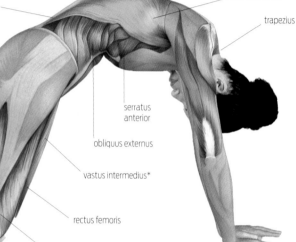

erector spinae*
multifidus spinae*
latissimus dorsi
trapezius
biceps femoris
serratus anterior
obliquus externus
vastus intermedius*
rectus femoris
vastus lateralis

Correct form
Fully engage your abdominals. Keep your arms and legs stable and lengthen your neck.

Avoid
Try not to arch only in your lower back or push down your ribcage.

Annotation Key
Bold text indicates target muscles
Black text indicates other working muscles
* indicates deep muscles

- Kneel on all fours with knees hip-width apart.
- Place your hands slightly ahead of your shoulders.
- Inhale and slowly curl your spine upward, tucking your head between your arms. Hold briefly.
- Exhale and curl your spine downward, arching your back.
- Hold and repeat 5 times.

221 Cat Roll-Up

The Cat Roll-Up is a great exercise for practicing how to articulate your spine. Control your breathing and move through the motions in a deliberate and flowing manner.

- Kneel on all fours with your back in neutral position.
- Inhale as you curl your spine upward and tuck in your head.
- Exhale as you open the front of your hips and continue curling up, lifting your hands from the mat and rolling up to a high kneeling position.
- Curl down to the starting position and repeat 5 times.

Benefits of back extensions
Extending the back muscles is the perfect antidote to excessive flexion in our daily lives—from sitting and bending forward to heavy lifting. Back extensions open the chest and hip flexors and increase mobility along the spine and in the hips.

222 Pointing Dog
Kneel on all fours with knees hip-width apart and hands under your shoulders. Press your navel to your spine and inhale. On exhale, lift your left arm and right leg to hip height. Reach your hand and foot outward. Lower and alternate arms and legs for a total of 10 repetitions.

223 Hydrant Lift with Band
Kneel on all fours and wrap a resistance band around your right shin. Hold the ends of the band under your left knee. Bend your right knee and rotate it out to the side. Lower and perform 10 repetitions on each leg.

224 Glute Press-Up
Kneel on all fours and wrap a resistance band around your right foot. Tuck the ends of the band under your left knee. Bend your right knee and lift your right foot toward the ceiling. Lower and perform 10 repetitions on each leg.

225

Breaststroke

The Breaststroke helps to realign your spine, especially in the upper and middle back. This exercise strengthens the scapular muscles around the shoulder blades as you rotate your arms, and it develops the extensor muscles as you hold yourself up. If you tend to slouch, the Breaststroke is a great exercise for you.

trapezius

supraspinatus*

infraspinatus*

teres minor

subscapularis*

rhomboideus*

latissimus dorsi

erector spinae*

quadratus lumborum*

Correct form
Your hip and pubic bones should remain on the mat. Squeeze your legs together. Align the back of your head and neck with your spine.

Avoid
Don't lift your torso any higher than the bottom of your ribcage.

Annotation Key
Bold text indicates target muscles
Black text indicates other working muscles
* indicates deep muscles

triceps brachii

gluteus maximus

semitendinosus

biceps femoris

semimembranosus

gastrocnemius

transversus abdominis*

rectus abdominis

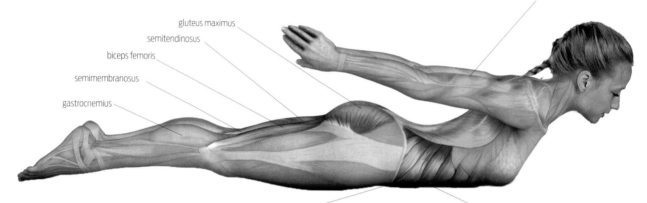

- Lie facedown with arms and legs extended. Inhale to prepare.
- Exhale as you lift your arms off the mat and reach forward.
- In a smooth, controlled manner, curl your upper chest from the mat and swing your arms around to the back.
- Bend your elbows to return to the front. Repeat 10 times.

226 Breaststroke with Balls

Lie facedown with legs together. Hold small weighted balls in each hand and extend your arms forward. Inhale to prepare. Perform the exercise as in the Breaststroke (#225). Repeat 5 times.

227 Superman

Lie facedown with arms and legs extended. Inhale and engage your abs. Exhale and lift your arms and legs from the mat, pulling them away from your torso. Hold for several breaths and lower. Repeat 5 times.

228 Swimming

Lie on your stomach with arms and legs extended, and inhale. Engage the abs and exhale as you raise your arms and legs. Begin to "flutter kick," pulsing the opposite arm and leg up and down. Inhale for 5 counts and exhale for 5 counts. Lower and repeat 3 times.

229 Swimming on Balance Ball

Support your hips on a balance ball. Perform the exercise as in Swimming (#228). Inhale for 5 counts and exhale for 5 counts. Lower and repeat 3 times.

230 Swan Dive

Lie on your stomach with feet shoulder-width apart and place your hands near your shoulders. Straighten your arms and lift your torso. Exhale as you bend your elbows and rock your torso downward, lifting your legs and sweeping your arms forward. As you rock back, return your arms to starting position. Repeat 5 times.

231 Swan Dive on Balance Ball

Support your hips on a balance ball. Place your hands on the floor under your shoulders. Inhale, bend your elbows, and rock your torso forward. Rock back, straightening your arms. Repeat 5 times.

232

Wide-Legged Plié

You don't need to be a
dancer to perform the
Wide-Legged Plié, which
tones your quads, inner
thighs, and glutes. The Plié
keeps your hip joints limber
and improves mobility in
your lower body.

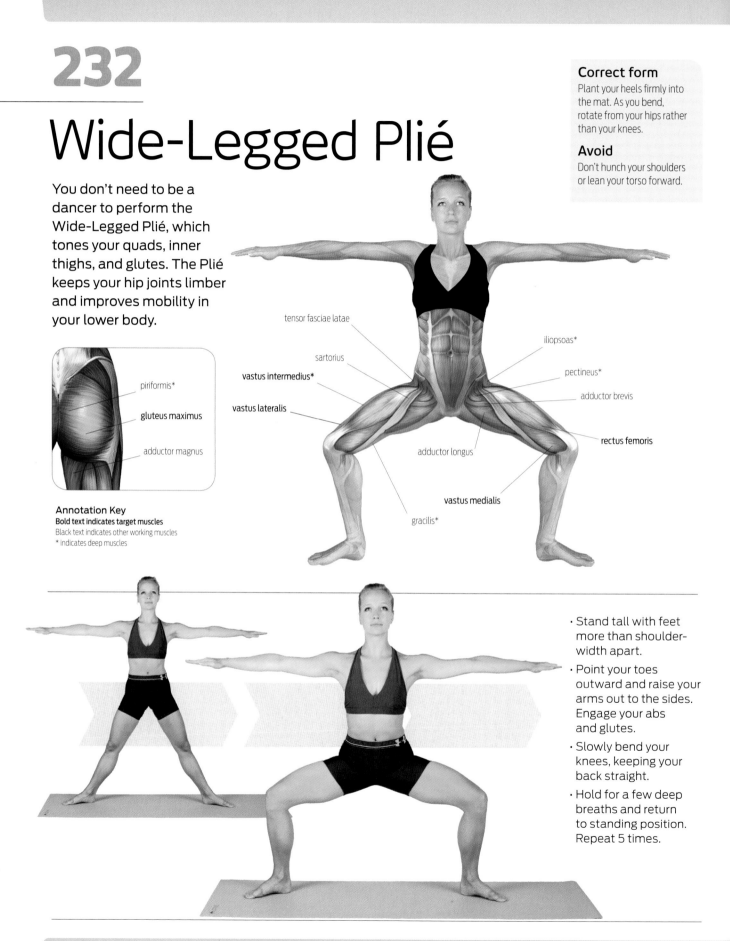

piriformis*

gluteus maximus

adductor magnus

Annotation Key
Bold text indicates target muscles
Black text indicates other working muscles
* indicates deep muscles

tensor fasciae latae

sartorius

vastus intermedius*

vastus lateralis

iliopsoas*

pectineus*

adductor brevis

rectus femoris

adductor longus

vastus medialis

gracilis*

- Stand tall with feet
  more than shoulder-
  width apart.
- Point your toes
  outward and raise your
  arms out to the sides.
  Engage your abs
  and glutes.
- Slowly bend your
  knees, keeping your
  back straight.
- Hold for a few deep
  breaths and return
  to standing position.
  Repeat 5 times.

233 Plié Squat

The Plié Squat is an easy way to improve mobility in your joints—from your hips down to your ankles.

- Stand with heels together and toes pointing out. Raise your arms in front of you to shoulder height.
- Engage your abs and glutes. Bend your knees, rotating from the hips. Keep your back straight.
- Hold for a few deep breaths and return to standing position. Repeat 5 times.

234 Wide Plié Tiptoes

Stand tall with feet more than shoulder-width apart. Lift onto tiptoes and raise your arms out to the sides. Perform the exercise as in the Wide-Legged Plié (#232). Repeat 5 times.

235 Plié with Heels Lifted

Stand tall and support your heels on small weighted balls about hip-width apart. Extend your arms in front of you and bend your knees outward, keeping your back straight. Repeat 5 times.

236 Tendon Stretch

Stand tall with feet together. Extend your arms forward. Engage your abs and glutes. Slowly bend from your hips, keeping your knees forward and your back straight. Hold for a few deep breaths and return to standing position. Repeat 5 times.

237 Tendon Stretch on Ball

Stand tall and support your heels on small weighted balls about hip-width apart. Extend your arms in front of you and bend your knees, keeping your back straight. Repeat 5 times.

Mermaid

The Mermaid stretches tight obliques and loosens up the shoulders. This exercise also engages the intercostals, the primary breathing muscles around your ribcage.

Annotation Key
Bold text indicates target muscles
Black text indicates other working muscles
* indicates deep muscles

rectus abdominis

obliquus externus

obliquus internus*

transversus abdominis*

infraspinatus*

teres major

latissimus dorsi

Correct form
Lengthen your spine and feel the energy release through your raised arm. Keep the lower hip grounded.

Avoid
Don't pop out your ribcage or arch your back.

- Sit with your knees bent and legs tucked at your left side. Inhale, place your left hand on your ankle, and extend your right arm upward.

- Exhale and bend your torso to your left. Reach your right arm overhead and gaze upward.

- Hold for several breaths. Repeat on the opposite side.

239 Mermaid with Circle

Sit with your knees bent and legs tucked at your left side. Place a magic circle at arm's length on your right. Extend your left arm overhead and bend to your right. Squeeze down on the circle. Return to the starting position and repeat 5 times per side.

240 Mermaid Tennis Serve

Sit with your knees bent and legs tucked at your left side. Hold a small weighted ball in your right hand and reach your hand behind you. Lift your right arm, as if preparing to serve a tennis ball, and circle it in front of you. Repeat 5 times before switching sides.

241 Knee Sway

Lie on your back with knees in tabletop position and arms out at your sides. Rotate your hips to the left, lowering your knees to the floor. Gaze in the opposite direction. Return to tabletop and repeat on the opposite side for a total of 10 repetitions.

242

Single-Leg Balance

The Single-Leg Balance stabilizes the core and strengthens the legs. Think of the Pilates principles of concentration, control, and flow to help you maintain your balance with correct posture. As you perform this exercise, imagine lengthening your spine upward.

Annotation Key
Bold text indicates target muscles
Black text indicates other working muscles
* indicates deep muscles

adductor magnus

rectus abdominis

Correct form
Stabilize your powerhouse and lengthen your spine. Control the leg extensions, pushing through the heel.

Avoid
Don't rock your hips or bend your torso.

obliquus externus

tensor fasciae latae

vastus lateralis

biceps femoris

adductor longus

tibialis anterior

rectus femoris

extensor digitorum longus

sartorius

vastus medialis

gastrocnemius

extensor hallucis

flexor hallucis*

- Stand straight and bend your left knee, lifting it to hip height. Straighten your leg forward.
- Bend your knee and extend your leg to the side. Next, bend your knee and extend your leg behind you.
- Perform the series 5 times on each leg.

243 Standing Leg Extension

Stand straight with hands on your hips. Engage your abs and open your chest. Bend your right knee to hip height, flex your foot, and extend your leg forward. Bend your knee and repeat the leg extension 5 times on each leg.

244 Balance on Tiptoe

Stand straight with feet together. Engage your abs and inhale. Lift up onto tiptoes and raise your arms overhead. Press your legs and heels together for balance. Hold for several breaths. Lengthen your spine and pull the energy from your toes, legs, and up your spine. Lower and repeat 5 times.

245 Balance Extension on Tiptoe

Stand straight with feet together. Engage your abs, raise your arms overhead, and inhale. Lift your right foot onto tiptoes and extend your left leg behind you, keeping your back straight. Hold for several breaths, lower, and repeat 5 times on each leg.

246 Standing Saw

Stand straight with feet more than shoulder-width apart and arms out at your sides. Curl your spine as you lower and twist your torso to the left. Touch your right hand to your left foot. Curl your back up and repeat on the opposite side for 10 repetitions per side.

247 Windmill

Stand straight with your feet hip-width apart. Inhale and engage your abs. Curl your head forward and slowly articulate your spine as you bend forward. Try to reach your hands to your toes. Hold for a few breaths and curl back up. Repeat 5 times.

248 Standing Extensions

Stand straight with feet together and arms on your hips. Extend your right leg behind you, pointing your toes. Hold for a few breaths and lower. Repeat 10 times on each leg.

249 Standing Cross Crunch

Stand with feet about hip-width apart and knees bent. Hinge forward slightly from your hips. Inhale, lift your left arm, and extend your right leg behind you. Exhale as you bring your back leg forward, touching your left elbow to your right knee. Alternate sides and perform 10 times per side.

250 Standing Twist

Stand straight with feet more than hip-width apart and arms extended out to the sides. Keeping your back straight and shoulders down, slowly twist to your left. Return to center and twist to your right. Repeat 10 times on each side.

251 Standing Arm and Leg Extensions

Improve your balance and mobility in your joints while stretching your spine. Reach with your arms and legs to feel the energy release from your limbs.

- Stand with feet together and knees bent. Hinge forward slightly from your hips.
- Lift your left arm and extend your right leg behind you.
- Return to the starting position. Alternate arms and legs for a total of 10 repetitions.

252

Shoulder Press with Weights

The Shoulder Press with Weights works your upper body, particularly the deltoids, triceps, and trapezius. The weight-bearing movement also helps to improve stability in the shoulders, elbows, and wrists.

triceps brachii
deltoideus anterior
biceps brachii
pectoralis major

levator scapulae*
supraspinatus*
deltoideus posterior
infraspinatus*
teres minor
subscapularis*
teres major

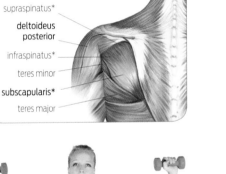

Annotation Key
Bold text indicates target muscles
Black text indicates other working muscles
* indicates deep muscles

- Stand straight with feet together and hold small weights in each hand.
- Inhale and bend your elbows to 90 degrees so your upper arms are parallel to the floor.
- Exhale and extend your arms overhead, keeping your shoulders down.
- Return to the bent-elbows position and repeat 10 times.

253 Shoulder Raise with Weights

Stand straight with feet together and hold small weights at your sides. Inhale and engage your abs, keeping your back neutral. Exhale as you lift your arms out to the sides and to shoulder height, with palms facing down. Lower and repeat 10 times.

254 Shoulder Raise Knee-Lift

Stand straight with feet together and hold small weights at your sides. Inhale and engage your abs, keeping your back neutral. Exhale as you lift your right knee to hip height and raise your left arm out to the side, palm facing down. Lower and repeat 10 times on each side.

255 Diagonal Arm Extension

Stand straight with feet hip-width apart and wrap a resistance band under your left foot. Hold the ends of the band in each hand at your left hip and inhale. Pull the band with your right hand diagonally upward. Lower and repeat 10 times on each side.

256 90-Degree Raise

Sit on a bench with small weighted balls in each hand. Rest your forearms on your thighs, palms facing up, and inhale. On exhale, hinge your arms out to the sides, keeping your elbows bent at 90 degrees. Lower and repeat 10 times.

257 Shoulder Rotator Raise

Sit on a bench with small weighted balls in each hand. Bend your elbows 90 degrees and raise them to shoulder height. Rotate your forearms up, lower, and repeat 10 times.

258 Peek-a-Boo

Sit on a bench with small weighted balls in each hand. Bend your elbows 90 degrees and lift your hands close to your face, pressing your forearms together. Pivot your shoulders open, maintaining the angle in your elbows and forming a straight line between elbows. Lower and repeat 10 times.

259 Shoulder Press-Up

Sit on a bench with small weighted balls in each hand. Bend your elbows 90 degrees and raise your elbows to shoulder height. Lift your hands overhead, lower, and repeat 10 times.

260 Chest Press with Circle

Sit on a bench and hold a magic circle in front of your chest. Press and hold for a few breaths. Release and repeat 10 times.

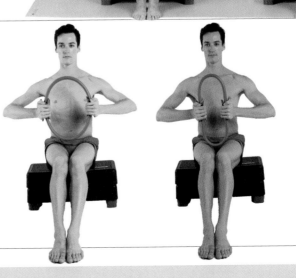

261

Back Extension

The Back Extension exercise is great for targeting your biceps and triceps. It also develops the erector spinae muscles along your spine. The Back Extension strengthens your chest muscles as well, giving your upper body a balanced workout.

Annotation Key
Bold text indicates target muscles
Black text indicates other working muscles
* indicates deep muscles

supraspinatus*
deltoideus posterior
infraspinatus
teres minor
teres major
rhomboideus*
latissimus dorsi

trapezius
triceps brachii
brachialis
brachioradialis
pectoralis major
serratus anterior
biceps brachii

Correct form
Control your movements and squeeze your shoulder blades together to keep them stable.

Avoid
Don't pop out your ribcage or arch your lower back.

- Stand with feet hip-width apart and knees bent. Hold a small weight in each hand and extend your arms forward, palms facing in, at about hip height.
- Hinge your torso forward. Bend your elbows and pull your arms back so your hands are close to your chest.
- Lower your arms and repeat 10 times.

262 Reverse Hug

Stand with feet hip-width apart and knees bent. Hold a small weight in each hand. Bring your hands together, palms facing down, at about hip height. Hinge your torso forward. Raise your arms out to the sides up to shoulder height. Lower your arms and repeat 10 times.

263 Row with Band

Sit on the floor with legs forward and wrap a resistance band around your feet. Hold the ends of the band in each hand and bend your elbows at your sides. Pull straight back on the band, release, and repeat 10 times.

264 Straight-Arm Row with Band

Sit on a mat with legs forward and wrap a resistance band around your feet. Hold the ends of the band in each hand above your knees. With your arms straight, pull the band out to the sides, keeping your hands close to the floor. Release and repeat 10 times.

265 High-Elbow Row with Band

Sit on the floor with legs forward and wrap a resistance band around your feet. Hold the ends of the band in each hand just above your knees. Lift your elbows out to the sides. Pull the band up to your chest, lower, and repeat 10 times.

266 Shoulder Rotator with Band

Sit on the floor with legs forward and wrap a resistance band around your feet. Hold the ends of the band in each hand just above your knees. Pressing your upper arms into your sides, pull on the band and rotate your shoulders and forearms outward. Release and repeat 10 times.

267 Single-Arm Row

Sit on a mat with legs forward and wrap a resistance band around your feet. Hold the ends of the band in each hand above your knees. Twist your torso to the left, pulling your elbow back. Return to center and twist to the right. Repeat 10 times to each side.

268

Overhead Triceps Press

The Overhead Triceps Press strengthens your triceps and lats and improves shoulder mobility. Strive for controlled movements without overextending. Start out using lighter weights, and as you gain strength, slowly build up to heavier weights.

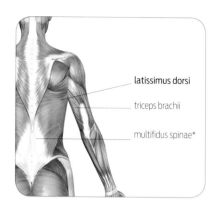

latissimus dorsi

triceps brachii

multifidus spinae*

Annotation Key
Bold text indicates target muscles
Black text indicates other working muscles
* indicates deep muscles

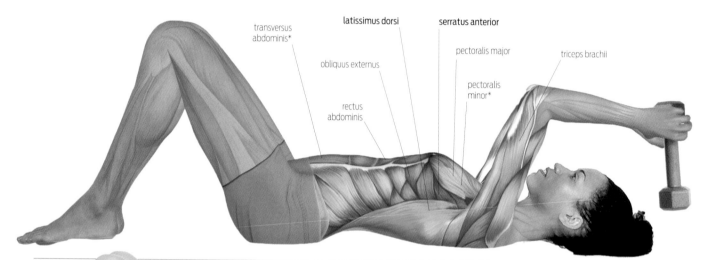

transversus abdominis*

latissimus dorsi

serratus anterior

obliquus externus

pectoralis major

triceps brachii

pectoralis minor*

rectus abdominis

Correct form
Move slowly and precisely. Try to isolate the stretch in your triceps.

Avoid
Don't shift your upper arms.

- Lie on a mat or a bench with knees bent. Hold a small weight with both hands overhead.

- Bend your elbows and keep them steady as you inhale and slowly lower the weight behind your head.

- Hold for a breath and exhale as you lift the weight overhead. Perform 10 repetitions.

269 Triceps Extension on Swiss Ball

Support your upper back on a Swiss ball with your knees bent. Hold light weights above your chest. Bend your elbows and lower your forearms parallel to the floor. Hold for a breath and exhale as you lift the weights upward. Repeat 10 times.

270 Pull-Over on Roller

Lie with a foam roller under your back and parallel to your body. Bend your knees. Hold a small weighted ball with both hands above your waist. Slowly raise your arms up and behind your head. Hold for a breath and return your arms to your waist. Perform 10 repetitions.

271 Triceps Press with Balls

Sit on a bench with feet together. Hold a small weighted ball in each hand and lift them just behind your head. In a controlled movement, extend your arms overhead with the balls touching throughout. Lower and repeat 10 times.

272 Triceps Press with Band

Sit on a mat with legs crossed. Hold a resistance band behind your back, with your left hand on the floor and your right hand overhead. Extend your right arm up, pulling on the band. Lower and repeat 10 times with each arm.

273 Triceps Kick Back

Kneel on all fours. Hold a light weight in your right hand. Bend your right elbow and lift the weight to your side. Extend your arm behind you, without locking the elbow, and lower to your side. Repeat 10 times on each arm.

274

Biceps Curl

The Biceps Curl may not be part of the classic Pilates repertoire, but it is an essential exercise for shoulder stabilization and very much a functional exercise. Considering all the daily lifting we do, the Biceps Curl should be part of everyone's Pilates routine.

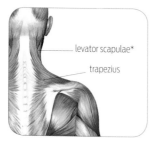

levator scapulae*

trapezius

Annotation Key
Bold text indicates target muscles
Black text indicates other working muscles
* indicates deep muscles

deltoideus anterior

biceps brachii

brachialis

brachioradialis

Correct form
Keep your elbows close to your body and your wrists stable throughout the movement.

Avoid
Avoid using momentum to lift the weights.

- Stand straight with a light weight in each hand and palms facing up. Keep your back in neutral position.

- Inhale as you slowly bend both elbows and reach your hands up toward your shoulders.

- Exhale and lower your hands to your sides. Repeat 10 times.

275 Advanced Biceps Curl

Challenge your balance with this harder variation of the basic Biceps Curl (#274). You'll give your core a workout too.

- Stand straight with a light weight in each hand and palms facing up.
- Engage your abs. Bend your left knee and raise it to hip height, flexing your foot.
- Perform as in the Biceps Curl (#274) for 5 repetitions. Repeat on the opposite leg.

276 Ballet Biceps

Stand straight with a light weight in each hand. Extend your arms out to the sides at shoulder height, elbows slightly bent and palms facing up. Inhale as you raise your hands overhead. Exhale and lower your hands to the starting position. Repeat 10 times.

277 Biceps Curl with Band

Sit on the floor and wrap a resistance band around your feet. Hold the ends of the band above your knees, palms facing up. Keep your elbows bent at 90 degrees as you pull the band up toward your face. Lower and repeat 10 times.

278 Biceps Curl with Balls

Sit on a bench with legs together. Hold small weighted balls at the sides of your knees. Perform the exercise as in the Biceps Curl (#274) for 10 repetitions.

279 Biceps Curl on Roller

Lie on a foam roller with legs together. Hold a small weighted ball in each hand outside your thighs. Curl the balls in toward your chest and lower. Repeat 10 times.

280 Biceps Curl with Squat

Stand with feet hip-width apart. Wrap a resistance band under your feet. Holding the ends of the band with palms facing up, bend your knees into a squat as you curl your arms in toward your chest. Return to the starting position and repeat 10 times.

281 Wrist Curl

Sit on a bench with legs together. Hold small weighted balls in each hand and rest your forearms on your thighs. With palms facing up, curl your wrists upward. Lower and repeat 10 times.

282 Wrist Hinge

The Wrist Hinge will help improve mobility in your wrists. They may also prevent and alleviate carpel tunnel syndrome by keeping your wrists limber and strong.

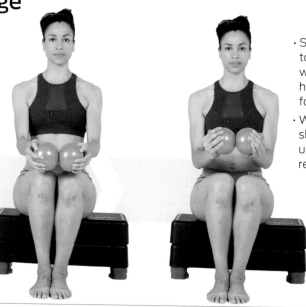

- Sit on a bench with legs together. Hold small weighted balls in each hand and rest your forearms on your thighs.
- With palms facing inward, slowly hinge your wrists upward. Lower and repeat 10 times.

283

Zipper

The Zipper is a multipurpose exercise that mimics the unzipping and opening of a jacket. You'll feel a stretch along the entire length your arms, from your wrists to your shoulders. The Zipper also strengthens your arms and chest while improving mobility in your shoulder and elbow joints.

Annotation Key
Bold text indicates target muscles
Black text indicates other working muscles
* indicates deep muscles

deltoideus medialis

triceps brachii

pectoralis major

Correct form
Use slow and controlled movements. Hold your arms up for a breath to feel the stretch along your inner arms.

Avoid
Don't tense your shoulders or neck.

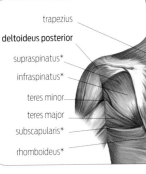

trapezius
deltoideus posterior
supraspinatus*
infraspinatus*
teres minor
teres major
subscapularis*
rhomboideus*

- Stand straight and hold light weights at your waist. Pull your shoulders down your back.
- Keep your wrists stable as you "zip" your hands down, straightening your arms, then lifting them out to the sides and up to shoulder height. Return to the starting position and repeat 10 times.

284 Single-Arm Circles

Stand straight with feet shoulder-width apart. Hold a small weighted ball in your right hand and place your left hand behind your back. Lift your right hand forward to shoulder height and circle your arm down and around. Perform 10 circles in each direction and alternate arms.

285 Double-Arm Circles with Balls

Stand straight with feet shoulder-width apart. Hold small weighted balls in each hand in front of you at shoulder height. Circle your arms simultaneously. Perform 10 circles in each direction.

286 Double-Arm Figure 8s

Stand straight with feet together. Hold a small weighted ball in each hand at your lower abdomen. Draw a small circle, bringing your hands out to the sides and up to your chest, then back out and overhead to complete the Figure 8. Reverse the order and repeat 5 times in each direction.

287 Arm Circles on Roller

Lie on a foam roller and bend your knees. Hold a small weighted ball in each hand and extend your arms overhead, parallel to the floor. Perform circles out to your sides and in toward your chest. Repeat 10 times.

288 Arm Raise on Roller

Lie on a foam roller and bend your knees. Hold a small weighted ball in each hand at your hips. Raise your arms overhead, perpendicular to the floor, and lower. Perform 10 arm raises.

289 Side-Lying Arm Lowers

Lie on your left side with your head propped up on your elbow. Bend your knees, forming a slight pike with your torso and legs. Hold a small weighted ball in your right hand at your hip and lift it straight up. Lower and repeat 10 times with each arm.

290 Side-Lying Arm Sweeps

Lie on your right side with your head propped up on your elbow. Bend your knees, forming a slight pike with your torso and legs. Hold a small weighted ball in your left hand in front of you. Sweep your arm behind you, return it to the front, and repeat 10 times with each arm.

291 Side-Lying Arm Circles

Lie on your left side with your head propped up on your elbow. Bend your knees slightly. Hold a small weighted ball in your right hand in front of you. Perform 10 circles in each direction. Repeat with the opposite arm.

292 Side-Lying Rotator Raise

Lie on your left side with your head propped up on your elbow. Bend your knees, forming a slight pike with your torso and legs. Hold a small weighted ball in your right hand on the mat. Pivot your elbow, raising your forearm. Return to the starting position and perform 10 arm raises. Repeat on the opposite arm.

293 Arm Raise on Swiss Ball

Lie on a Swiss ball with knees bent at 90 degrees. Hold a small weighted ball in each hand at your sides. With straight arms, raise your arms overhead and lower. Repeat 10 times.

294

Chest Fly

The Chest Fly mainly builds up the pecs, the primary chest muscles. But it also tones your biceps and delts. You can perform the Chest Fly on the floor or, for a deeper chest stretch, on a bench.

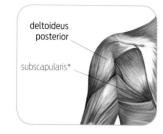

deltoideus posterior

subscapularis*

Annotation Key
Bold text indicates target muscles
Black text indicates other working muscles
* indicates deep muscles

Correct form
Tuck in your abs and keep your spine in a neutral position. Stabilize your shoulder blades during the movement.

Avoid
Don't swing your arms up using momentum.

- Lie on a mat or a bench with knees bent. Hold a small weight in each hand and extend your arms out to the sides.
- Inhale as you lift your arms straight up above your chest and hold for a breath.
- Slowly exhale and lower your arms out to the sides. Hold briefly and repeat 10 times.

pectoralis major

deltoideus anterior

coracobrachialis

biceps brachii

triceps brachii

295 Chest Press with Circle
Lie on a mat with knees bent. Hold a magic circle just above and parallel to your chest. Squeeze the circle, release. Lift your arms up about a foot, squeeze the circle, release. Extend your arms straight up, squeeze the circle, and release. Reverse direction and repeat 10 times.

296 Chest Press and Crunch

Lie on a mat with knees bent. Hold a magic circle just above your chest. Squeeze the circle as you curl your head and upper shoulders off the mat. Lower and repeat 10 times.

297 Chest Press and Oblique Crunch

Lie on a mat with knees bent. Hold a magic circle just above your chest. Squeeze the circle as you curl your head and shoulders off the mat and twist your torso to the right. Lower and crunch to the left. Repeat 10 times on each side.

298 Chest Fly on Roller

Lie on a foam roller and bend your knees. Hold 2 small weighted balls and extend your arms out to the sides. Inhale, lift the balls straight up above your chest, and press them together. Exhale and lower. Repeat 10 times.

299 Chest Fly on Swiss Ball

Lie on a Swiss ball and bend your knees. Hold 2 small weighted balls out at your sides. Inhale, lift the balls straight up above your chest, and press them together. Exhale and lower. Repeat 10 times.

300 Shoulder Stretch on Roller

Lie on a foam roller and bend your knees. Hold a small weighted ball with both hands and raise your arms above your chest. Roll the ball between your palms, stretching your right arm up while pulling your left arm down. Continue rolling up and down for several breaths.

CHAPTER TWO

Machine and Arc Barrel Exercises

The Pilates apparatuses may at first be intimidating—with their pulleys, straps, and bars—but the machines offer several advantages over regular mat work. Apparatuses such as the reformer and the Pilates chair use springs to add resistance to your movements—in both directions. You can customize the resistance, and you can build strength and stamina during the entire exercise. When working with spring-resistance equipment, remember that the more springs you use, the more resistance you will feel.

Another good piece of equipment that will add an extra dimension to your Pilates routine is the arc barrel. This piece of equipment allows you to lengthen the spine, or increase or decrease the challenge in each exercise.

"Change happens through movement, and movement heals."

—Joseph Pilates

301

Footwork on Toes

Footwork exercises are some of the most popular routines on the Pilates reformer. Also known as the Leg Press, this exercise stabilizes and aligns the ankles, knees, and hip joints while strengthening the core and leg muscles. Feel the lengthening in your quads and calves as you push from the foot bar.

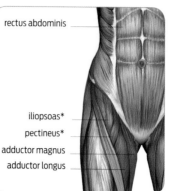

rectus abdominis

iliopsoas*
pectineus*
adductor magnus
adductor longus

Correct form
Relax the spine in neutral position. Control the movement and press your legs together, engaging your inner-thigh muscles.

Avoid
Don't kick off the bar and lose balance.

Annotation Key
Bold text indicates target muscles
Black text indicates other working muscles
* indicates deep muscles

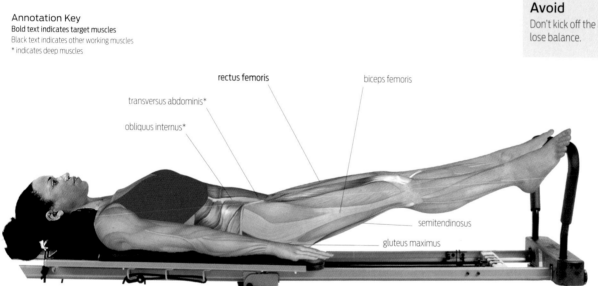

rectus femoris

biceps femoris

transversus abdominis*

obliquus internus*

semitendinosus

gluteus maximus

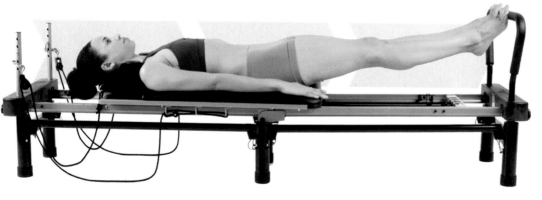

- Lie on a reformer with the headrest up. Place your toes parallel on the foot bar, heels together.
- Bend your knees and keep your arms flat at your sides.
- Keep the pelvis neutral. Inhale and press on the bar.
- Exhale and return to the bent-knees position. Repeat 10 times.

302 Footwork in V-Position

Lie on a reformer. Place your toes slightly apart on the foot bar, heels together, in the Pilates V-position. Bend your knees and place your arms at your sides. Inhale and press on the bar. Exhale and return to the bent-knees position. Repeat 10 times.

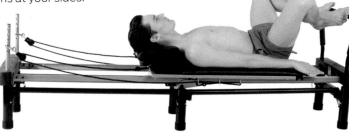

303 Seated Footwork on Toes

Sit toward the edge of a reformer platform with knees bent and toes on the foot bar. Relax your spine in a slight C-curve. Inhale, push out from the foot bar, and lengthen your spine. Exhale and return to the starting position. Repeat 10 times.

304 Single-Leg Footwork on Toes

Lie on a reformer and place your right toes on the foot bar. Bend your left knee in tabletop position and keep your pelvis neutral. Inhale and press on the bar, lengthening your right leg. Exhale and return to the bent-knees position. Repeat 10 times on each leg.

305 Seated Leg Press on Toes

Sit on a Pilates chair and place the balls of your feet on the pedals about hip-width apart. Rest your hands behind your back and engage your abs. Push down in quick but controlled movements, pulsing the pedals with your feet. Perform 20 repetitions.

306

Standing High Single-Leg Press

Place your left foot and both hands on the seat of a Pilates chair. Balance your right foot on the pedal and inhale. Exhale as you press down on the bar. Pulse 10 times on each foot.

307

Standing Single-Leg Press Sideways

Stand with your left side next to a Pilates chair. Place your hands behind your back. Press your left foot down on the pedal and pulse 10 times. Repeat on the opposite leg.

308

Straddle Press

Lie on a reformer with the headrest up. Bend your knees and place your feet in the straps. Extend your legs overhead, and in a controlled movement, lower your legs out to the sides. Return your legs overhead and repeat 10 times.

309

Windmill Leg Press

Lie on a reformer and place your feet in the straps. Extend your legs overhead and lower them out to the sides. Circle your left leg toward the foot bar, then circle your right leg to meet your left leg. Repeat 10 times, alternating legs.

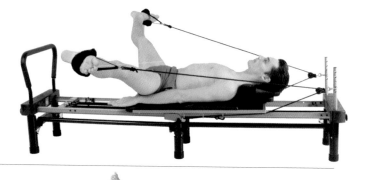
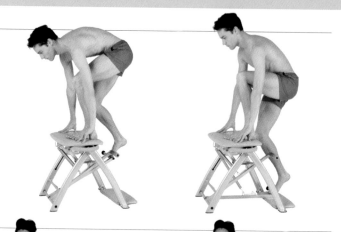

310 Kneeling Leg Press

Place your hands and left knee on the seat of a Pilates chair. Position your right foot on a pedal and pulse up and down 10 times. Repeat with the opposite leg.

311 Seated Frog Press

Sit on a Pilates chair with heels together and toes pointing out, in V-position. Place your hands behind your back and engage your abs as you push down on the pedals. Pulse up and down 10 times.

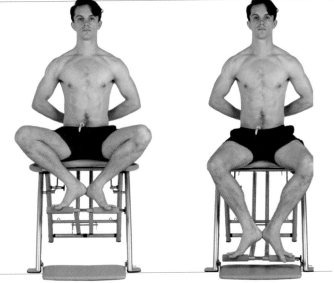

312 Seated Ski Pulse

Sit on a Pilates chair with legs and feet together. Place your toes on the pedals and rest your hands behind your back. Engage your abs and twist your knees to the right as you push down on the pedals. Lift your knees, twist them to the left, and push down on the pedals. Pulse 10 times to each side.

The Pilates chair

The Pilates chair is a compact but versatile machine with short and powerful springs. This apparatus builds strength and motor coordination. Once you start pumping the pedals, you'll also get a great cardio workout.

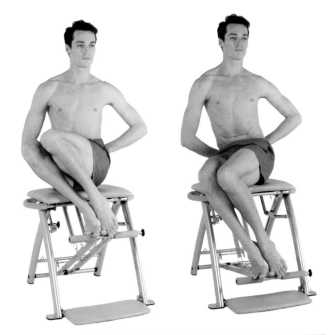

313

Footwork on Heels

The Footwork on Heels exercise is similar to Footwork on Toes, working the core and stabilizing the hips, knees, and ankles. But with the heels on the foot bar and feet flexed, you feel an added stretch in your shins and more lengthening in the hamstrings.

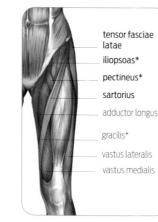

tensor fasciae latae
iliopsoas*
pectineus*
sartorius
adductor longus
gracilis*
vastus lateralis
vastus medialis

- Lie on a reformer and rest your heels on the foot bar.
- Bend your knees and place your arms at your sides.
- Keep the pelvis neutral and inhale. Press on the bar and straighten your legs.
- Exhale and return to the bent-knees position. Repeat 10 times.

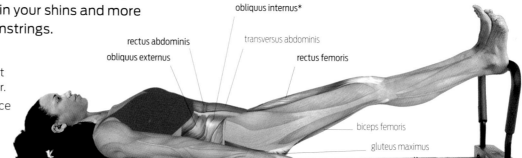

obliquus internus*
rectus abdominis
obliquus externus
transversus abdominis
rectus femoris
biceps femoris
gluteus maximus

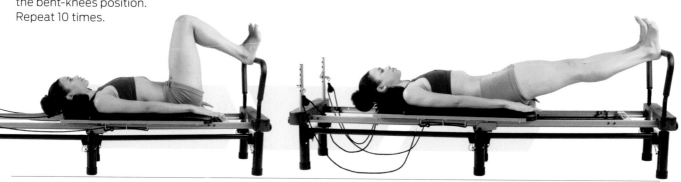

314

Footwork on Wide Heels
Lie on a reformer and place your heels wide apart on the foot bar. Point your toes outward and bend your knees. Keep your pelvis neutral and inhale. Press on the foot bar and straighten your legs. Exhale and return to the bent-knees position. Repeat 10 times.

315

Seated Single-Leg Press on Heels

Sit on a Pilates chair with your right leg extended forward and left heel on the pedal. Place your hands behind your back and engage your abs. Push down on the pedal and pulse 10 times. Repeat on the opposite leg.

316

Standing Single-Leg Press on Heels

Stand facing a Pilates chair. Place your right heel on a pedal and rest your hands behind your back. Engage your abs as you push down on the pedal and pulse 10 times. Alternate legs and repeat.

317

Reformer Calf Raise

Lie on a reformer with the headrest down. Rest the arches of your feet on the bar and flex your feet. Straighten your legs. Slowly roll your toes forward, then return to the starting position. Repeat 10 times.

318

Seated Leg Press on Heels

Sit on a Pilates chair with your heels on the pedals and toes pointing forward. Keep your legs parallel and place your hands behind your back. Engage your abs and push down on the pedal. Pulse 10 times.

319

Seated Leg Press with Heels Wide

Sit on a Pilates chair with heels wide on the pedals, toes pointing outward and knees wide. Place your hands behind your back and engage your abs. Engage your abs and push down on the pedal. Pulse 10 times.

320

Basic Jumping

The explosive movements of Basic Jumping offer a vigorous cardio workout. Plyometrics, or jump training, develops strength and range of motion with low impact on the joints. It involves coordinating three types of extension: in the ankles, knees, and hips. Jump board jumping builds that explosive power essential to so many sports.

Correct form
Keep your hips stable. As you jump off, roll your feet from heel to toe; when landing, roll down from toe to heel.

Avoid
Don't land on your heels or slam into the jump board.

Annotation Key
Bold text indicates target muscles
Black text indicates other working muscles
* indicates deep muscles

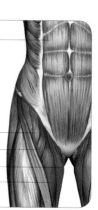

rectus abdominis

iliopsoas*
pectineus*
adductor magnus
adductor longus

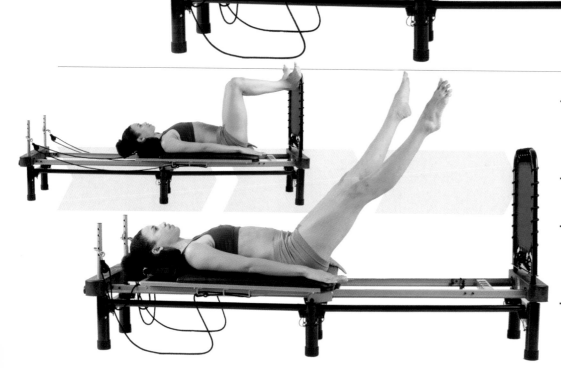

rectus femoris

transversus abdominis*

obliquus internus*

semimembranosus

biceps femoris

semitendinosus

gluteus maximus

gluteus medius*

- Lie on a reformer with a jump board attached. Bend your knees and place your feet hip-width apart on the jump board.

- Push off, articulating your feet and straightening your legs.

- As you return, bend your knees and bring the platform close to the jump board to engage the core muscles.

- Repeat 10 times.

321 Jump Board Hopping

Add some hopping to your jump board routine to work on your coordination and hip flexibility. As you hop, push off with equal force from both feet.

- Lie on a reformer with the headrest down. Place your right foot on the jump board and lift your left leg in tabletop.
- Push off with your right foot, rolling from heel to toe. Land on your left foot from toe to heel.
- Continue hopping for 10 repetitions on each foot.

322 Jumping with Feet Together

Lie on a reformer with the headrest down. Bend your knees and place your feet on the jump board. Press your legs together. Push off the board and straighten your legs. As you return, bend your knees. Repeat 10 times.

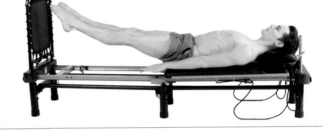

323 Jumping V-Feet

Lie on a reformer with the headrest down. Bend your knees and place your feet on the jump board with heels together and toes out in V-position. Push off the board and straighten your legs. As you return, bend your knees. Repeat 10 times.

324 Jump Board Skiing

Lie on a reformer with the headrest down. Place your feet hip-width apart on the jump board, bend your knees, and twist them to the left. Push off the board and straighten your legs. Twist to the right and bend your knees as you return. Repeat 10 times.

325 Jump Board Calf Raise

Lie on a reformer and place your feet on the jump board, keeping your legs straight. Press your legs together and articulate your heels from the board. Slowly roll your heels down. Repeat 10 times.

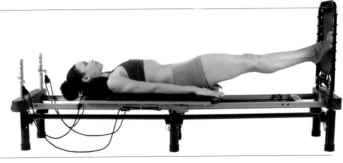

326

Reformer Leg Lowers

Reformer Leg Lowers help to develop stability in the pelvis and lower back. This exercise also strengthens the hip adductors and extensors as well as the hamstrings. Focus on the Pilates principles of centering and flow as you perform these Leg Lowers to improve balance and flexibility in the hips.

Annotation Key
Bold text indicates target muscles
Black text indicates other working muscles
* indicates deep muscles

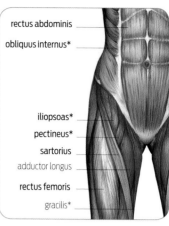

rectus abdominis
obliquus internus*
iliopsoas*
pectineus*
sartorius
adductor longus
rectus femoris
gracilis*

Correct form
Engage your abs and breathe laterally. Keep your legs aligned with your hips as you move through the motions.

Avoid
Don't pop out your ribcage as you lower your legs.

tensor fasciae latae

biceps femoris

transversus abdominis*

obliquus externus

gluteus maximus

gluteus medius*

- Lie on a reformer with the headrest down. Place your feet in the straps and extend your legs toward the ceiling.
- Press your legs together. Slowly lower your legs, keeping them straight.
- Return to the starting position and repeat 10 times.

327 Diamond Lowers in Straps

Lie on a reformer with the headrest down. Place your feet in the straps and press your heels together. Point your toes outward and let your knees drop to shoulder-width apart. Slowly lower your legs, keeping your knees bent. Return to the starting position and repeat 10 times.

328 Leg Lowers with Thighs in Straps

Lie on a reformer with the headrest down. Place the straps around your thighs and bend your knees in tabletop position. Press your legs together. Slowly lower your feet close to the floor. Return to the starting position and repeat 10 times.

329 Leg Lowers Supported

Lie on a reformer with the headrest down. Hold on to the shoulder pads for support and raise your legs straight up. Engage your abs and slowly lower your legs, keeping them straight. Return to the starting position and perform 10 repetitions.

330 Bent-Leg Lowers on Pedal

Lie on the floor with your heels resting on the pedals of a Pilates chair. Flex your feet. Push down with your right heel, return, and push down with your left heel. Repeat 10 times with each foot.

Frog Bent-Leg Lowers on Pedal

Lie on the floor with your heels resting on the pedals of a Pilates chair. Flex your feet. Point your toes out and push down with your right heel. Return and push down with your left heel. Repeat 10 times with each foot.

Bent-Arm Leg Lowers

Lie on the floor with your shoulders resting on the foot cushion of a Pilates chair. Hold on to the pedals and raise your legs toward the ceiling. Engage your abs and slowly lower your legs to 45 degrees from the floor. Return to the starting position and repeat 10 times.

Leg Lowers on Arc Barrel

Lie with your back on an arc barrel. Rest your hands on the sides of the barrel. Extend your legs straight up and press them together. Slowly lower your legs, keeping them straight. Return to the starting position and repeat 10 times.

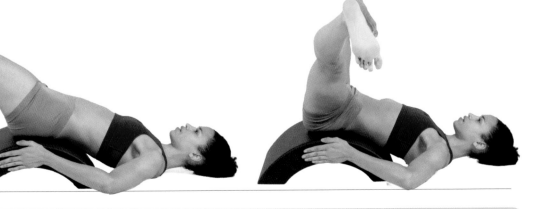

334 Diagonal Leg Lowers

Lie with your back on an arc barrel. Rest your hands on the sides of the barrel. Extend your legs straight up and press them together. As you slowly lower your legs, twist them to the left. Return to the starting position and twist to the right. Repeat 10 times on each side.

335 Diamond Leg Lowers on Arc Barrel

Lie with your back on an arc barrel. Extend your legs up and press your heels together with toes pointing out. Let your knees drop to shoulder-width apart and slowly lower your legs. Return to the starting position and repeat 10 times.

336 Straddle Press on Barrel

Lie with your back on an arc barrel. Extend your legs up and press your heels together with toes pointing out. Engage your abs and lower your legs straight out to the sides. Return to the starting position and repeat 10 times.

337

Reformer Leg Circles

Reformer Leg Circles work the core and all the leg muscles, including the hard-to-reach inner and outer thighs. Leg Circles improve flexibility in the hamstrings and hip flexors. The wider you draw your circles, the more challenging your workout.

Annotation Key
Bold text indicates target muscles
Black text indicates other working muscles
* indicates deep muscles

rectus abdominis

iliopsoas*

pectineus*

adductor magnus

adductor longus

Correct form
Engage your abs and stabilize your pelvis. Press your tailbone into the platform.

Avoid
Don't rock your torso or hips. Avoid arching your back.

rectus femoris

transversus abdominis*

biceps femoris

semitendinosus

gluteus maximus

obliquus internus*

- Lie on a reformer with the headrest down. Put your feet in the straps and raise your legs straight up.
- Lower your legs out to the sides, circle them forward, and press your legs together.
- Return to the starting position. Switch direction and repeat 10 times in each direction.

338 Windmill Circles in Straps

Windmill Circles on the reformer require a bit of coordination and flexibility, as you circle your legs in opposite directions.

- Lie on a reformer and place your feet in the straps. Raise your legs straight up.
- Scissor your right leg toward your torso, and your left leg toward the foot bar. Circle both legs out and back up.
- Scissor your legs in the opposite direction and repeat 10 times in each direction.

339 Leg Circles with Chair

Lie on the floor with your hands on the pedals of a Pilates chair. Lift your legs toward the ceiling. Circle your legs outward, then forward, and back up. Repeat in the opposite direction and perform 10 circles in each direction.

340 Single-Leg Circles in Straps

Lie on a reformer with the headrest down. Place your left foot on the bar. Put your right foot in a strap and extend your leg straight up. Lower your leg out to the side and circle it forward and back. Perform 10 circles with each leg.

341 Leg Circles Supported

Lie on a reformer and hold on to the shoulder pads. Extend your legs straight up. Lower your legs out to the sides, circle them toward the floor, and press your legs together. Return to the starting position. Switch direction and repeat 10 times in each direction.

342 Leg Circles on Arc Barrel

Lie down with your lower back on an arc barrel. Extend your legs straight up. Lower your legs out to the sides, circle them down toward the floor, and press your legs together. Return to the starting position. Switch direction and repeat 10 times in each direction.

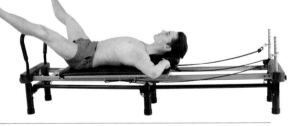

343

Reformer Crunch

Get six-pack abs with the Reformer Crunch. This exercise targets the four main abdominal muscles: the transversus abdominis, rectus abdominis, and the internal and external obliques. As you work the pulleys, you also strengthen your arms and shoulders.

- Lie on a reformer with legs in tabletop.
- Hold the straps and extend your arms overhead as you inhale.
- Exhale as you curl your head and shoulders from the platform and pull your arms down to your sides.
- Inhale and return to the starting position. Repeat 10 times.

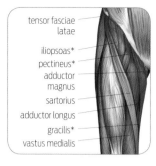

tensor fasciae latae
iliopsoas*
pectineus*
adductor magnus
sartorius
adductor longus
gracilis*
vastus medialis

Correct form
Articulate your spine as your roll up and roll back down. Stabilize your pelvis and press your legs together.

Avoid
Don't tense your neck or change your leg position.

Annotation Key
Bold text indicates target muscles
Black text indicates other working muscles
* indicates deep muscles

obliquus internus*

rectus abdominis

obliquus externus

pectoralis major

deltoideus anterior

teres major   biceps brachii

vastus lateralis

rectus femoris

vastus intermedius*

transversus abdominis*

344 Crunch with Thigh Straps

Lie on a reformer with legs in tabletop. Wrap the straps around each thigh and place your hands behind your head. Exhale and curl your head and shoulders as you pull your knees in toward your chest. Inhale and return to the starting position. Repeat 10 times.

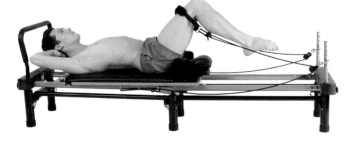

345 Oblique Crunch with Straps

Lie on a reformer with legs in tabletop. Wrap the straps around each thigh and extend your hands overhead. Exhale, curl your head and shoulders up, and twist your torso to the right, reaching your arms to your side. Lower and repeat to the other side for a total of 10 repetitions.

346 Seated Crunch

Sit on a Pilates chair and reach your hands down to the pedals. Lift your knees up and inhale. On exhale, push down on the pedals. Return to the starting position and repeat 10 times.

347 Seated Teaser Crunch

Sit on a Pilates chair and reach your hands down to the pedals. Lift your knees and extend your legs into Teaser. On exhale, push down on the pedals. Return to the starting position and repeat 10 times.

348 Seated Diagonal Crunch

Sit on a Pilates chair and reach your hands down to the pedals. Lift your knees and extend your legs into Teaser, twisting them slightly to the left. On exhale, push down on the pedals. Return to the starting position and repeat to the opposite side for a total of 20 repetitions.

349 Hundred on Reformer

Lie on a reformer with legs in tabletop. Wrap the straps around your feet. Exhale and extend your legs to 45 degrees. As you curl your head and shoulders up, pulse your arms up and down. Inhale for 5 counts, and exhale for 5 counts. Perform for 20 counts.

350

Reformer Spine Twist

Correct form
Initiate the movement from your abs. Lengthen your spine upward and stretch your arms out to the sides.

Avoid
Don't use momentum to twist; control the movements.

The Reformer Spine Twist increases the range of motion in the upper body and stretches the length of the spine. The twisting motion lengthens the obliques and develops a leaner torso. Imagine releasing energy from your hands as you pull your arms in opposite directions.

Annotation Key
Bold text indicates target muscles
Black text indicates other working muscles
* indicates deep muscles

deltoideus

flexor digitorm*

extensor digitorum

triceps brachii

teres major

latissimus dorsi

erector spinae*

quadratus lumborum*

rectus femoris

tensor fasciae latae

gluteus maximus

biceps femoris

- Sit on a reformer with your feet on the bar. Bring your arms forward at shoulder height.
- Push off the bar as you twist your torso to the left and extend your arms out to the sides.
- Return to the starting position and repeat to the right. Perform 10 repetitions to each side.

351 Spine Twist Kneeling

Kneel on a reformer and hold a strap on your right side. Twist your upper body to the left, maintaining stability in your hips. Repeat 10 times on each side.

352 Standing Saw

Stand at the side of a Pilates chair with your arms out to the sides. Twist your torso to the right. With your left hand, push down on the pedal. Return to the standing position and repeat 10 times on each side.

353 Oblique Cross-Over

Kneel facing a Pilates chair. Place your left hand on the pedal and extend your right arm to the side. Twisting your torso to the right, push down on the pedal. Repeat 10 times and alternate sides.

354 Hula on Arc Barrel

Sit on an arc barrel with knees bent and feet off the floor. Extend your arms for balance. Press your legs together and twist your torso to the right while twisting your legs to the left. Return to the center and perform to the opposite side. Repeat 10 times in each direction.

355 Roll-Back Obliques

Sit on a reformer with your feet on the headrest. Hold the straps close to your chest with your elbows out to the sides. Lean back and twist your torso to the left. Return to the center and repeat to the right. Perform 10 repetitions to each side.

356

Single-Leg Stretch on Arc Barrel

The Single-Leg Stretch on Arc Barrel develops the stabilizer muscles of your core and spine. The Pilates principles of centering and balance come into play here as you engage your abs, balance on the barrel, and move your legs fluidly back and forth.

Annotation Key
Bold text indicates target muscles
Black text indicates other working muscles
* indicates deep muscles

rectus femoris

semimembranosus

trapezius

serratus anterior

biceps femoris

semitendinosus

rectus abdominis

obliquus internus*

latissimus dorsi

transversus abdominis*

obliquus externus

gluteus maximus

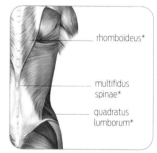

rhomboideus*

multifidus spinae*

quadratus lumborum*

- Lie with your lower back on an arc barrel. Curl your head and neck up. Bring your legs into tabletop.

- Extend your right leg forward as you bring your left knee in toward your chest. Rest your hands on your bent leg for balance.

- Alternate legs and repeat 5 times on each leg.

357 Hip Flexor Stretch on Arc Barrel

Lie with your lower back on an arc barrel and shoulders on the floor. Rest your right foot on the floor. Bend your left knee and gently pull it in toward your chest. Alternate legs for 5 repetitions on each leg.

358 Forward Lunge on Chair

Stand facing a Pilates chair. Place your left foot on the seat of the chair, and your right foot on a pedal. Rest your hands behind your back and push down on the pedal for 5 repetitions. Alternate legs and repeat.

359 Hamstring Stretch on Reformer

Lie on a reformer with the headrest down. Place your right foot in a strap and your left toes on the bar. Hold for several breaths to feel the stretch. Repeat on the opposite leg.

360 Outer-Thigh Stretch on Reformer

Lie on a reformer with the headrest down. Place your right foot in a strap and your left toes on the bar. Stretch your right foot down toward your left side, keeping the knee straight. Hold for several breaths and repeat on the opposite leg.

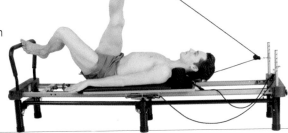

361 Inner-Thigh Stretch on Reformer

Lie on a reformer with the headrest down. Place your left foot in a strap and your right toes on the bar. Stretch your left foot out to your left side, keeping the knee straight. Hold for several breaths and repeat on the opposite leg.

362

Double-Leg Stretch on Arc Barrel

The Double-Leg Stretch on Arc Barrel requires core strength and coordination. Move slowly through this exercise, not only to maintain your balance but also to engage your abs fully. Reach your arms and legs away from your torso and feel the energy release through your hands and feet.

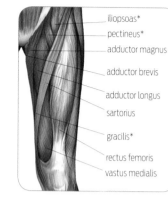

iliopsoas*
pectineus*
adductor magnus
adductor brevis
adductor longus
sartorius
gracilis*
rectus femoris
vastus medialis

Correct form
Engage your abs throughout, pulling your ribcage toward your hip bones. Keep your gaze on your knees.

Avoid
Don't bob your head up and down during the exercise.

Annotation Key
Bold text indicates target muscles
Black text indicates other working muscles
* indicates deep muscles

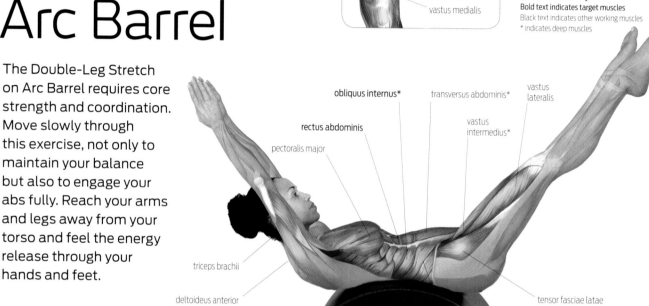

obliquus internus*
transversus abdominis*
vastus lateralis
rectus abdominis
vastus intermedius*
pectoralis major
triceps brachii
deltoideus anterior
tensor fasciae latae
obliquus externus

- Lie on an arc barrel. Bring your knees into tabletop and curl your head and neck up. Place your hands on your knees and inhale.
- As you exhale, slowly extend your arms and legs out to 45 degrees.
- Swing your arms down and back. Return to the starting position and repeat 5 times.

363 Double-Leg Stretch on Chair
Lie with your shoulders on the footrest of a Pilates chair. Hold the pedals and curl your head and neck up. Bring your legs into tabletop and inhale. On exhale, extend your legs to 45 degrees. Return your legs to tabletop and repeat 10 times.

364 Bicycle on Arc Barrel

Balance your middle back on an arc barrel with your legs in tabletop. Clasp your hands behind your head and curl up. Twist to your left as you straighten your right leg to 45 degrees and bring your left knee into your chest. Bicycle to the opposite side for 10 repetitions per side.

365 Scissors on Hips

Balance your lower back on an arc barrel with your shoulders and head on the floor. Bring your legs into tabletop and extend them upward. Scissor your legs by alternating one leg up and one leg down. Perform 10 repetitions per leg.

366 Scissors on Back

Balance the middle of your back on an arc barrel and extend your legs straight up. Curl your head off the floor and alternate moving one leg up and one leg down in the scissors movement. Find your balance by touching the raised leg. Perform a total of 10 repetitions per leg.

367 Scissors with Chair

Lie with your shoulders on the footrest of a Pilates chair. Hold the pedals for balance and curl your head and neck up. Bring your legs into tabletop and alternate moving one leg up and one leg down in the scissors movement. Perform a total of 10 repetitions per leg.

368 Crisscross with Chair

Lie with your shoulders on the footrest of a Pilates chair. Hold the pedals for balance and curl your head and neck up. Bring your legs into tabletop and inhale. On exhale extend your legs to 45 degrees from the floor. Crisscross your legs, over and under each other, for 10 counts.

369

Reformer Frog Press

The Reformer Frog Press challenges your core, glutes, and inner thighs. This exercise helps to develop stability in your hip flexor muscles and improves flexibility in your knees and ankles.

Correct form
Keep your spine neutral rather than imprinting into the platform. Keep your tailbone pressed down.

Avoid
Don't bring your knees too far in toward your chest.

Annotation Key
Bold text indicates target muscles
Black text indicates other working muscles
* indicates deep muscles

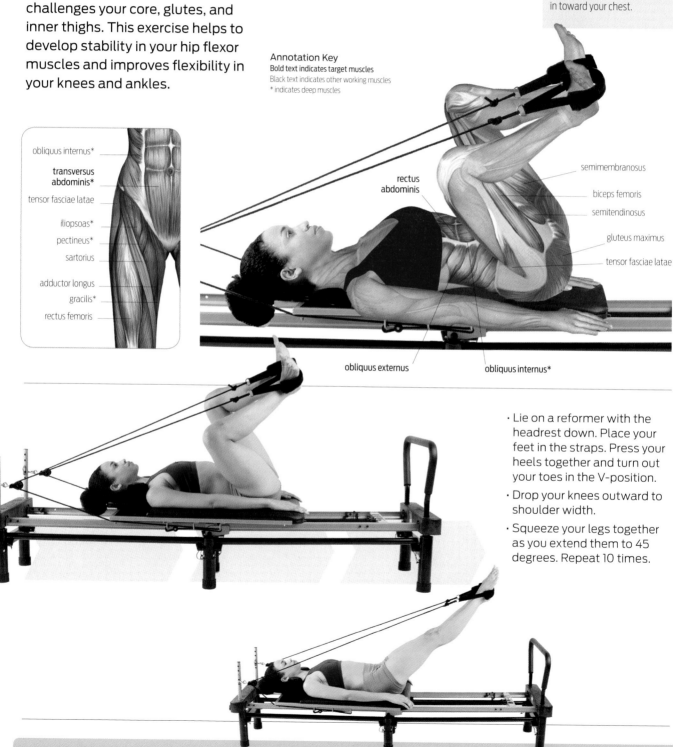

obliquus internus*
transversus abdominis*
tensor fasciae latae
iliopsoas*
pectineus*
sartorius
adductor longus
gracilis*
rectus femoris

rectus abdominis

semimembranosus
biceps femoris
semitendinosus
gluteus maximus
tensor fasciae latae

obliquus externus
obliquus internus*

- Lie on a reformer with the headrest down. Place your feet in the straps. Press your heels together and turn out your toes in the V-position.
- Drop your knees outward to shoulder width.
- Squeeze your legs together as you extend them to 45 degrees. Repeat 10 times.

370 Reformer Frog Circles

Lie on a reformer and place your feet in the straps. Press your heels together, turn out your toes, and lower your knees to your sides. Hinge your legs open and circle your legs around and forward to 45 degrees. Squeeze your legs together and repeat 5 times.

371 Frog C-Curve

Sit on a Pilates chair and rest your feet on the pedals, heels together and toes apart in V-position. Hold the armrests and curl your head and upper back into a C-curve as you push down on the pedals. Pulse 5 times with your feet.

372 Frog Short Spine

Lie on a reformer with your feet in the straps. Press your heels together and turn out your toes. Bend your knees and lift your legs overhead as you curl your back from the platform. Find your balance and extend your legs to 45 degrees. Slowly lower, articulating your spine, and repeat 5 times.

373 Elephant Frog

Stand on a reformer at the shoulder pads and place your hands on the foot bar. Slowly push away from the bar, keeping your pelvis stable, and return to the starting position. Repeat 5 times.

374 Frog Press on Arc Barrel

Lie down with your lower back on an arc barrel and shoulders on the floor. Lift your legs into frog position, pressing your heels together. On exhale, straighten your legs at a diagonal and squeeze your legs together. Return to the starting position and repeat 5 times.

375

Jackknife on Arc Barrel

The Jackknife on Arc Barrel is a slightly easier version of the Jackknife. So if your powerhouse isn't that strong yet, the extra support of the barrel will give you a boost and help you find your balance. Focus on lengthening through your spine and your legs.

biceps femoris

gluteus maximus

vastus lateralis

rectus femoris

tensor fasciae latae

transversus abdominis*

obliquus internus

gluteus medius*

obliquus externus

rectus abdominis

iliopsoas*

pectineus*

sartorius

gracilis*

rectus femoris

vastus lateralis

Annotation Key
Bold text indicates target muscles
Black text indicates other working muscles
* indicates deep muscles

brachioradialis

biceps brachii

triceps brachii

deltoideus

- Lie with your lower back supported on an arc barrel and shoulders on the floor. Extend your legs up and inhale.
- On exhale, slowly curl your back from the barrel, extending your legs diagonally overhead.
- Hold for a few breaths, slowly lower, and repeat 5 times.

376 Jackknife on Reformer

Lie on a reformer with your feet on the bar. Hold the straps. As you pull your arms down to your sides, curl your back up and lift your feet overhead so your legs are parallel to the floor. Raise your legs to 45 degrees, hold for a breath, and lower. Repeat 5 times.

377 Jackknife Scissors

Lie on a reformer with your feet on the bar. Holding the shoulder pads for support, curl your back off the platform and lift your legs overhead to Jackknife. Perform the scissors movement by lowering one leg and raising the other leg. Alternate legs for 5 counts.

378 Jackknife Supported

Lie on a reformer with feet on the bar. Holding the shoulder pads, curl your back from the platform and roll your legs overhead, parallel to the floor. Lift your legs up into Jackknife. Hold for a breath, lower, and repeat 5 times.

379 Jackknife Obliques

Lie on a reformer and hold the shoulder pads for support. Curl your back off the platform and roll your legs overhead into Jackknife. Squeeze your legs together as you twist your hips to the right and lower your legs diagonally. Alternate sides and repeat 3 times on each side.

380 Short Spine on Reformer

The Short Spine on Reformer is a great workout for anyone with a stiff lower back or tight hamstrings. A heavier spring setting will help release your tight muscles.

- Lie on a reformer with feet in the straps. Press your heels together and lower your legs to 45 degrees.
- Slowly bring your legs overhead as you curl your back off the platform.
- Bend your knees in toward your chest, lower your hips, and push your feet back upward into diagonal. Repeat 5 times.

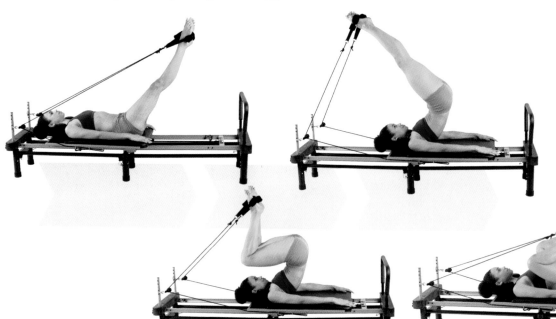

381 Long Spine on Reformer

Lie on a reformer with feet in the straps. Press your heels together and lower your legs to 45 degrees. Slowly bring your legs up overhead as you curl your back off the platform. Open your legs slightly, lower your hips and legs, and return to the starting position. Repeat 5 times.

382 Rollover on Arc Barrel

Lie with your back on an arc barrel and shoulders on the floor. Extend your legs up and press them together. Roll your back off the barrel and bring your legs overhead, parallel to the floor. Flex and open your feet slightly, and touch your toes to the floor. Lower and repeat 5 times.

383 Rollover on Reformer

Lie on a reformer and hold the straps at your sides. Lift your legs straight up. Curl your back off the platform and extend your legs overhead, parallel to the floor. Flex and open your feet slightly, hold for a breath, and return to the starting position. Repeat 5 times.

384 Rollover Supported

Lie on a reformer and hold the shoulder pads for support. Lift your legs straight up. Curl your back off the platform and extend your legs overhead, parallel to the floor. Flex and open your feet slightly, hold for a breath, and return to the starting position. Repeat 5 times.

385 Reverse Curl in Straps

Lie on a reformer with your legs in tabletop. Wrap the straps around your thighs. Keeping your knees bent, curl your back off the platform. Hold for a breath and return to the starting position. Repeat 10 times.

386 Reverse Curl with Arms Stable

Lie on a reformer and hold the straps at your sides. Bend your knees in toward your chest and curl your back off the platform. Hold for a breath and return to the starting position. Repeat 10 times.

387

Arc Barrel Corkscrew

The Arc Barrel Corkscrew gives the abdominal obliques a tough workout. The Corkscrew improves spinal rotation while helping to stabilize the shoulders, as you keep your upper body still and rotate your legs in circles. As with all Pilates exercises, the Arc Barrel Corkscrew develops your core muscles.

Correct form
Inhale as you initiate the circling away from your body. As you bring your legs back toward your torso, exhale to scoop in your abdominals.

Avoid
Don't lower your legs so far that your lower back lifts from the barrel.

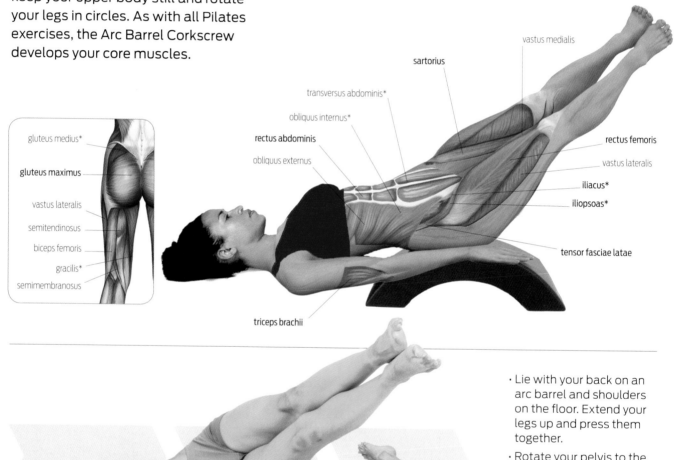

gluteus medius*
gluteus maximus
vastus lateralis
semitendinosus
biceps femoris
gracilis*
semimembranosus

sartorius
vastus medialis
transversus abdominis*
obliquus internus*
rectus abdominis
obliquus externus
rectus femoris
vastus lateralis
iliacus*
iliopsoas*
tensor fasciae latae
triceps brachii

- Lie with your back on an arc barrel and shoulders on the floor. Extend your legs up and press them together.
- Rotate your pelvis to the right, following with your legs. Circle down toward the floor, toward the left, and back up.
- Reverse direction and repeat 5 times in each direction.

388 Reformer Corkscrew

The Reformer Corkscrew is a slightly harder version of the Arc Barrel Corkscrew. You need to harness all your powerhouse muscles to rotate your pelvis and lift your hips as you circle your legs.

- Lie on a reformer and hold the straps at your sides. Extend your legs up and press them together.
- Inhale as you twist your pelvis to the right, following with your legs. Circle downward, lowering your hips to the platform.
- Rotate your pelvis to the left, and back up.
- Reverse direction and repeat 5 times in each direction.

389 Corkscrew Supported

Lie on the reformer and hold on to the shoulder pads. Extend your legs up and press them together. Perform the exercise as in the Reformer Corkscrew (#388) and repeat 5 times in each direction.

390 Corkscrew with Chair

Lie down with your head on the footrest of a Pilates chair. Hold on to the chair and lift your legs straight up. Engage your abs. Rotate your pelvis to the left, following with your legs. Circle your legs clockwise and repeat in the opposite direction.

391 Tick Tock

Lie down with your head on the footrest of a Pilates chair. Hold on to the chair and lift your legs straight up. Engage your abs and tilt your pelvis to the right, following with your legs. Return to the center and repeat to the left. Perform 10 repetitions.

392

Teaser on Reformer

The Teaser on Reformer is a demanding full-body workout that requires balance, precise control, and a lot of core strength. Focus on opening the chest and lengthening the spine while keeping a slight curve in the lower, lumbar spine.

Annotation Key
Bold text indicates target muscles
Black text indicates other working muscles
* indicates deep muscles

Correct form
Articulate the spine as you curl up and roll back down. Stabilize your pelvis and maintain a slight curve in your lower back.

Avoid
Don't arch your back or pop out your ribcage.

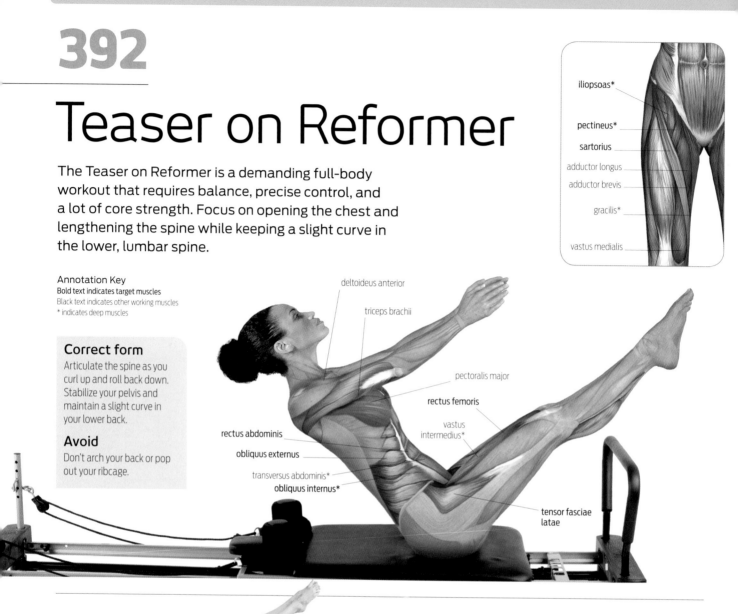

iliopsoas*
pectineus*
sartorius
adductor longus
adductor brevis
gracilis*
vastus medialis

deltoideus anterior
triceps brachii
pectoralis major
rectus femoris
vastus intermedius*
rectus abdominis
obliquus externus
transversus abdominis*
obliquus internus*
tensor fasciae latae

- Lie on a reformer with your calves on the foot bar. Extend your arms out to the sides and inhale.
- Curl your head and neck from the platform. As you exhale, raise your legs to 45 degrees and sweep your arms up and parallel to your legs.
- Hold for a breath, lower, and repeat 5 times.

393 Single-Leg Teaser

The Single-Leg Teaser is a slightly easier variation because one leg remains on the foot bar for support. Try to hold the V-position for several breaths to work your powerhouse.

- Lie on a reformer with your calves on the foot bar. Extend your arms out to the sides and inhale.
- As you exhale, curl your head and neck from the platform and raise your right leg to 45 degrees.
- Sweep your arms up diagonally. Hold for a breath, lower, and repeat 2 to 3 times on each leg.

394 Teaser on Diagonal

Lie on a reformer with your calves on the right side of the foot bar. Extend your arms out to the sides and inhale. As you exhale, curl your back up and sweep your arms up diagonally. Hold for a breath, lower, and repeat 5 times per side.

395 Teaser on Arc Barrel

Lie with your back on an arc barrel and feet on the floor. Inhale and extend your legs to 45 degrees. Slowly curl your head and neck from the floor. As you exhale, sweep your arms up and parallel to your legs. Hold for a breath, lower, and repeat 5 times.

396 Teaser Pulse on Arc Barrel

The Teaser Pulse on Arc Barrel requires quite a bit of balance and strength, but it's a simpler version of the Teaser because you begin from a seated position rather than curling up from the floor.

- Sit on an arc barrel and lift your legs into tabletop position. Extend your arms forward and inhale.
- As you exhale, straighten your legs to 45 degrees, and lean your torso back slightly, forming a V with your torso and legs.
- Pulse your arms up and down for 5 counts.

397 Teaser Twist to Pike

Sit on a Pilates chair and reach your right hand to the pedal behind you. Raise your legs to 45 degrees and extend your left arm in front of you. Push down on the pedal as you twist onto your right hip and reach your left arm overhead. Repeat 2 or 3 times on each side.

398 Teaser to Extension

Lie on a reformer. Hold the straps and lift your legs into tabletop. Curl your head and upper back from the platform and straighten your legs to 45 degrees, forming a V with your torso and legs. Lower and repeat 5 times.

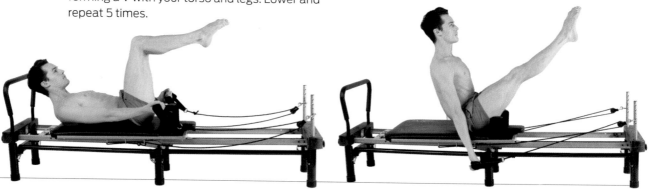

399

Plank on Chair

The Plank on Chair isolates your shoulder and arm muscles as you work one side of your body at a time. This demands a coordinated effort to stabilize your spine and pelvis so you don't twist your torso through the motion. The Plank on Chair builds shoulder strength and flexibility.

Annotation Key
Bold text indicates target muscles
Black text indicates other working muscles
* indicates deep muscles

Correct form
Keep your spine aligned throughout the exercise. Move fluidly with precise, controlled movements.

Avoid
Don't hunch your shoulders or let your pelvis droop.

deltoideus medialis
deltoideus anterior
pectoralis minor*
pectoralis major
biceps brachii
obliquus internus*
rectus abdominis
transversus abdominis*
vastus intermedius*
rectus femoris
vastus medialis*
tibialis anterior

trapezius
triceps brachii
serratus anterior
erector spinae*
gluteus maximus
biceps femoris
coracobrachialis*
obliquus externus
vastus lateralis

- Kneel at the side of a Pilates chair. Place your right hand on a pedal and assume the High Plank position.
- Keep your torso and hips stable as you push the pedal down with your right hand. Slowly pulse up and down 5 to 10 times.
- Repeat on the opposite side.

400 Push-Ups on Arc Barrel

Kneel beside an upside-down arc barrel. Place your hands on the sides of the barrel. Inhale and lift yourself up so your shoulders are in line with your hands. As you exhale, bend your elbows and lower your chest to the barrel. Repeat 10 times.

401 Plank Push-Down

Kneel beside a Pilates chair. Place your left hand on the seat, bending your elbow, and put your right hand on a pedal. Extend your legs into a High Plank. Keep your body stable as you push the pedal down with your right hand. Pulse up and down for 5 repetitions. Alternate sides and repeat.

402 Push-Up Push-Down

Kneel beside a Pilates chair. Place your left hand on the seat, and your right hand on a pedal. Extend your arms and legs into a High Plank position (#156). Push the pedal down with your right hand, lowering your body. Return to the High Plank, and repeat 5 times on each side.

403 Split-Pedal Push-Down

Kneel beside a Pilates chair. Place each hand on a pedal. Assume a High Plank position (#156) with straight arms. Push the pedals down, one at a time, for 10 repetitions.

404 Low Plank with Raised Legs

Kneel with your feet near a Pilates chair.
Place your feet on the pedals and assume
a Low Plank position (#134)
on your forearms.
Hold for 5 counts.

405 Plank Leg Lowers

Kneel with your feet near a Pilates chair.
Place your feet on the pedals and
assume a Low Plank position (#134)
on your forearms.
Push down
on the pedals
and repeat 5 times.

406 Pedal Push-Up

Kneel with your feet near a
Pilates chair. Place your feet
on the pedals and assume
a High Plank position (#156)
with extended arms. Keeping
your feet stable, lower your
chest to the floor
and perform 10
Push-Ups (#198).

Quality trumps quantity

In the world of Pilates, you're not likely to hear a question like "How many
Push-Ups can you do?" That's because in Pilates, quantity doesn't matter nearly
so much as quality. A few Push-Ups that are perfectly executed Pilates-style—
with precise control, an aligned spine, an engaged core, deep lateral breathing,
and fluid movement—would beat 100 sloppy Push-Ups any day.

407

Pike on Chair

The Pike on Chair is a challenging exercise that requires balance and strength. It's an effective workout that targets all the major muscle groups. Because the Pike is inverted, it works some supporting muscles that may otherwise get underused.

Annotation Key
Bold text indicates target muscles
Black text indicates other working muscles
* indicates deep muscles

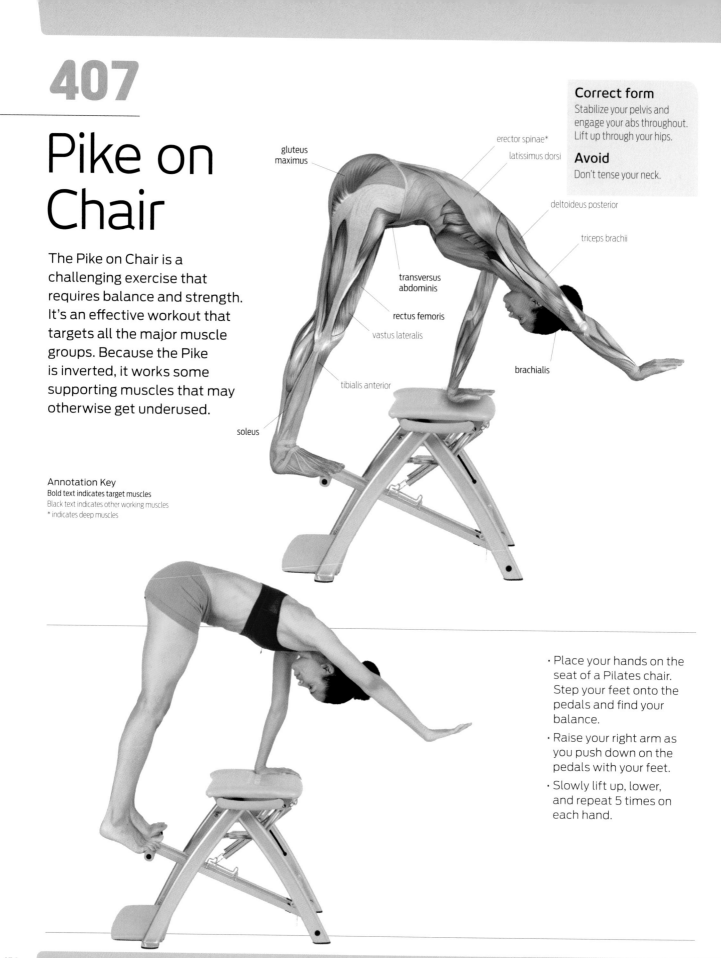

gluteus maximus

erector spinae*

latissimus dorsi

deltoideus posterior

triceps brachii

transversus abdominis

rectus femoris

vastus lateralis

brachialis

tibialis anterior

soleus

- Place your hands on the seat of a Pilates chair. Step your feet onto the pedals and find your balance.
- Raise your right arm as you push down on the pedals with your feet.
- Slowly lift up, lower, and repeat 5 times on each hand.

408 Pike Pull-Up

The Pike Pull-Up demands concentration and precise movements. You may feel a bit unstable at first, but if you can focus on your abs to lift your hips, your legs will follow too.

- Place your hands on the seat of a Pilates chair. Step your feet onto the pedals and find your balance.
- Engage your abs to lift your hips upward, letting your legs float up with the pedals.
- Slowly lower and repeat 10 times.

409 Pike with Split Pedal

Place your hands on the seat of a Pilates chair. Step your feet onto the pedals and find your balance. Alternate lifting one foot at a time on the pedals. Perform 10 times on each foot.

410 Pike-Up Oblique

Place your hands on the seat of a Pilates chair. Step your feet onto the pedals and find your balance. Engage your abs to lift your hips upward, letting your legs float up with the pedals.

411 Single-Leg Pike

The Single-Leg Pike requires stability in the pelvic area. If you're not entirely comfortable with balancing in this position, raise your leg only slightly until you gain confidence and strength.

- Place your hands on the seat of a Pilates chair.
- Step your left foot onto the pedal and lift your right leg out to the side.
- Find your balance, engage your abs, and lift your hips upward.
- Perform 5 repetitions on each leg.

412 Pike Down

Kneel in front of a Pilates chair. Place your feet onto the pedals and assume the inverted V-position. Engage your abs and lift your hips. Slowly lower and repeat 10 times.

413 Snake Down

Kneel in front of a Pilates chair. Place your feet onto the pedals and assume the inverted V-position. Cross your left foot behind the right, engage your abs, and lift your hips. Slowly lower and repeat 10 times.

414 Push-Downs

Stand facing a Pilates chair with feet hip-width apart. Curl your back down and place your hands on the pedals. Push the pedals down to the floor, return to starting position, and repeat 10 times.

415

Arc Barrel Arch-Ups

Arc Barrel Arch-Ups help to improve your posture and spinal stability. This exercise also strengthens your deep abs and back muscles. Performing Arch-Ups on an arc barrel offers you a greater range of motion than simply performing this exercise on a mat.

Correct form
Position your hips on top of an arc barrel. Lengthen your spine as you pull your limbs away from your torso.

Avoid
Don't arch your back or lift your arms or legs too high.

Annotation Key
Bold text indicates target muscles
Black text indicates other working muscles
* indicates deep muscles

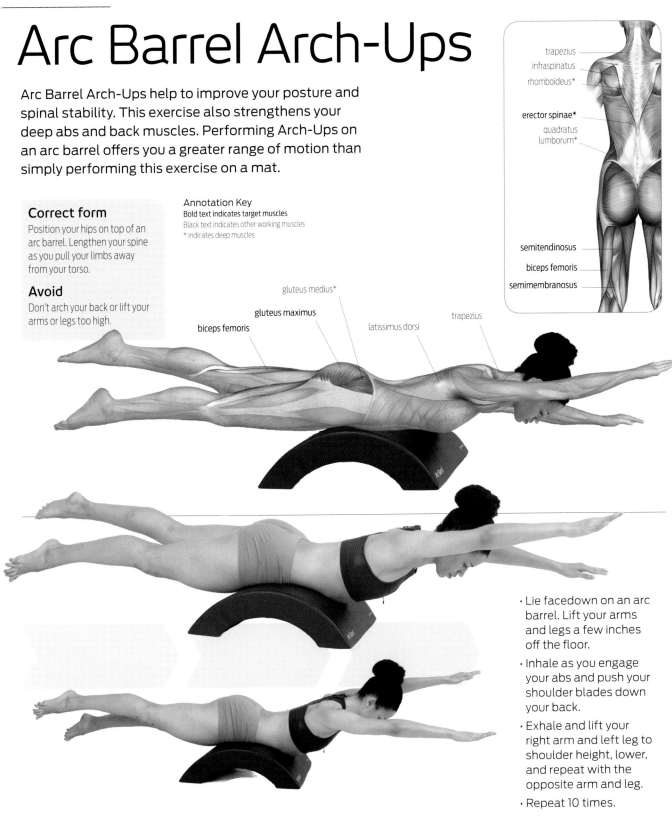

trapezius
infraspinatus
rhomboideus*
erector spinae*
quadratus lumborum*
semitendinosus
biceps femoris
semimembranosus

gluteus medius*
gluteus maximus
biceps femoris
latissimus dorsi
trapezius

- Lie facedown on an arc barrel. Lift your arms and legs a few inches off the floor.
- Inhale as you engage your abs and push your shoulder blades down your back.
- Exhale and lift your right arm and left leg to shoulder height, lower, and repeat with the opposite arm and leg.
- Repeat 10 times.

416 Quick Swim on Barrel

Lie facedown on an arc barrel. Extend your arms and legs, and inhale. Engage your abs and push your shoulder blades down your back. Exhale and lift both arms and legs to shoulder height. Lower your left arm and right leg, and flutter kick for 5 counts on inhale and 5 counts on exhale.

417 Seal Heel Clicks

Lie facedown on an arc barrel. Place your palms on the floor under your shoulders. Lean your torso forward and lift your legs to 45 degrees from the floor. Point your toes and turn them outward. Tap your heels together 10 times and lower your legs. Perform 3 sets.

418 Arch-Up Extensions

Lie facedown on an arc barrel. Extend your arms and legs, and inhale. Engage your abs and pull your shoulder blades down your back. Exhale and lift your arms and legs to shoulder height. Hold for 5 counts, lower, and repeat 3 times.

419 Rocking on Barrel

Lie facedown on an arc barrel. Place your palms on the floor under your shoulders and lift up your chest. Engage your abs and pull your shoulder blades down your back. Bend your elbows and rock your legs up behind you. Rock back and repeat 10 times.

420 Swan Twist

Position your hips on top of a Pilates chair. Inhale and push the pedal down with your right hand. Lower your left arm to the floor and raise your legs parallel to the floor. Exhale as you raise the right pedal and twist your torso open and to the left. Repeat 10 times on each side.

421 Swan on Chair

Position your hips on top of a Pilates chair. Push down on the pedals with your hands and raise your legs parallel to the floor. Exhale as you raise the pedals and lift your torso. Open your chest and elongate your spine. Repeat 10 times.

422 Arm Pulses Prone

Position your hips on top of a Pilates chair. Place your left hand on the pedal and bend your elbow. Extend your right arm out to the side. Lift your legs to hip height. Exhale and pulse the pedal up and down 5 times. Repeat with the opposite arm.

Back extensions

So many of our daily movements involve spinal flexion, or bending the body forward. Extension, on the other hand, arches the spine backward and opens the chest. As you perform extension exercises, elongate your spine by imagining that your limbs are pulling away from your body and feel the energy release from your fingertips and toes.

Rocking on Chair

Position your hips on top of a Pilates chair. Place your hands on the pedals and lift your legs parallel to the floor. Exhale as you push the pedal down and let your legs rock upward. Lower and repeat 5 times.

Split-Pedal Arm Press

Position your hips on top of a Pilates chair. Place your hands on the pedals and lift your legs parallel to the floor. Push down on the pedal with your right hand, lift, then push down with your left hand. Repeat 5 times with each hand.

Single-Arm Pedal Raise

Position your hips on top of a Pilates chair. Push the pedal down with your left hand and extend your right arm out to the side. Lift your legs parallel to the floor. Slowly raise the left pedal. Push down and repeat 5 times with each hand.

426 Twisted Swan Press

Position your left hip on top of a Pilates chair. Place both hands on the pedals and raise your legs to hip height. Push down on the pedals. Lift back up and repeat 5 times on each side.

427 Swan Press Prone

Lie facedown in front of a Pilates chair. Position your feet hip-width apart and place your hands on the pedals. Inhale to prepare. Exhale as you push down on the pedals and curl your torso up from the floor, keeping your gaze forward. Release and repeat 5 times.

428 Split-Pedal Swan

Lie facedown in front of a Pilates chair with feet hip-width apart. Inhale and place your hands on the pedals. Exhale as you push down on the right pedal and turn your gaze to the right. Alternate sides and repeat 10 times.

What's in a gaze?

In Pilates, correct form is essential, and where you focus your eyes also impacts your form. When you gaze upward, you engage your neck extensors; when you gaze downward, you use your neck flexors. Let your eyes guide your body as you move through the exercises with flow and precision.

429

Bridge on Tiptoe

Bridge on Tiptoe strengthens the glutes, hamstrings, and quads and works wonders for pelvic stability. It also develops the back extensors, which can improve your posture. A stronger backside will relieve lower-back pain too.

erector spinae*

multifidus spinae

gluteus medius
gluteus minimus

gluteus maximus

adductor magnus

semitendinosus

biceps femoris

semimembranosus

Correct form
Move slowly and deliberately, pushing evenly through your hips. Exhale on the extension and inhale as you lower.

Avoid
Don't pop out your ribcage.

Annotation Key
Bold text indicates target muscles
Black text indicates other working muscles
* indicates deep muscles

biceps femoris

gluteus maximus

rectus abdominis

gastrocnemius

- Lie on a reformer with the headrest down and arms at your sides.
- Bend your knees and place your toes parallel on the foot bar.
- Articulate your spine from the platform as you straighten your legs.
- Hold for a breath and slowly curl back down. Repeat 5 times.

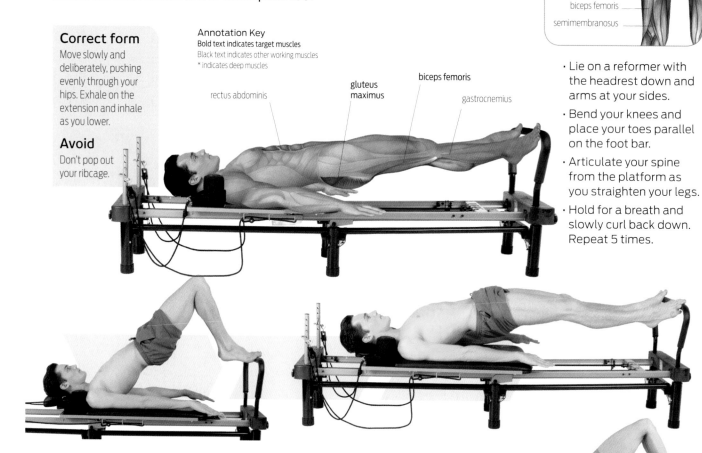

430

Bridge on Arches
Lie on a reformer with the headrest down and arms at your sides. Bend your knees and place your arches on the foot bar with feet parallel. Keeping the platform stable and your knees bent, articulate your spine up from the platform. Hold for a breath and slowly curl back down. Repeat 5 times.

431

Bridge in V-Position

Lie on a reformer with the headrest down and arms at your sides. Bend your knees and place your feet on the foot bar. Press your heels together and point your toes outward. Slowly curl your hips and lower back from the platform as you straighten your legs. Hold for a breath and slowly curl back down. Repeat 5 times.

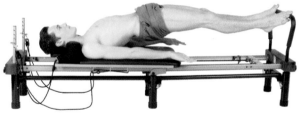

432

Bridge with Wide Feet

Lie on a reformer with the headrest down and arms at your sides. Bend your knees and place your heels on the foot bar about shoulder-width apart. Slowly curl your hips and lower back from the platform as you straighten your legs. Hold for a breath and curl back down. Repeat 5 times.

433

Bridge with Leg Kick

Lie on a reformer with knees bent and feet on the foot bar. Slowly curl your hips and lower back from the platform. As you straighten your legs, lift your left leg up to 45 degrees. As you bring the platform back in, lower your left leg toward the bar. Repeat 5 times and alternate legs.

434

Bridge Pulse

Lie on a reformer with knees bent and toes on the foot bar. Curl up from the platform, keeping your knees bent. Lift your left leg and tap it on the foot bar 5 times. Repeat with the other leg.

435

Bridge on Chair

Lie on your back with your heels resting on the pedals of a Pilates chair. Curl your hips and back from the floor into Bridge position. Press down on the pedals, one foot at a time. Perform 5 repetitions with each foot.

436

Side Double-Leg Lifts on Arc Barrel

Correct form
Try to form a straight line from your head down to your feet. Stabilize your shoulder blades.

Avoid
Don't let your torso droop toward the floor.

Side Double-Leg Lifts on Arc Barrel improve your balance and posture and build up your stamina. This exercise also strengthens your obliques, hips, and upper arms. Be conscious of keeping your whole body in proper alignment and move with controlled precision.

biceps brachii

rectus abdominis

deltoideus anterior

obliquus internus*

transversus abdominis*

obliquus externus

deltoideus posterior

erector spinae*

latissimus dorsi

Annotation Key
Bold text indicates target muscles
Black text indicates other working muscles
* indicates deep muscles

- Lie with your left hip on an arc barrel and place your left forearm on the floor. Rest your right arm along your side.
- Press your heels and legs together and inhale to prepare.
- Exhale as you lift your legs to hip height. Hold for a breath and lower.
- Repeat 5 times on each side.

437 Side Staggered-Leg Lifts

Lie with your right hip on an arc barrel and place your right forearm on the floor. Raise your left leg to hip height. Lift your right leg to meet your left leg, lower, and repeat 5 times on each side.

438 Side Scissors

Lie with your right hip on an arc barrel and place your right forearm on the floor. Rest your right hand on your hip. Engage your abs and inhale. Exhale as you lift your legs to hip height and move one leg forward and one leg back. Continue the scissors motion for 5 counts.

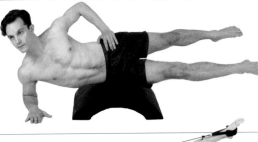

439 Side Leg Lowers on Reformer

Lie on your right side on a reformer. Place a strap on your left foot and bend your right knee. Rest your left hand by your chest. Lift your left leg up toward the ceiling. Lower your leg and repeat 10 times on each leg.

440 Side Leg Circles on Reformer

Lie on your right side on a reformer. Place a strap on your left foot and bend your right knee. Rest your left hand by your chest. Lift your left leg up toward the ceiling and circle your leg 10 times. Repeat on the right leg.

441 Side Leg Sweeps on Reformer

Lie on your right side on a reformer. Place a strap on your left foot and bend your right knee. Rest your left hand by your chest. Lift your left leg up to hip height and sweep it forward and back. Repeat 10 times on each leg.

442 Side Arch-Ups on Chair

Position your left hip on a Pilates chair. With your left hand, push down on the pedal. Place your right hand behind your head. Lift your legs to hip height and press them together. Bend your torso upward and release the pressure on the pedal. Push down and repeat 5 times on each side.

443

Hamstring Stretch

The Hamstring Stretch does just what its name suggests: It stretches out the muscles in the back of the leg. Tight hamstrings may contribute to pain in the lower back and behind the knee, and they can pull the pelvis out of alignment. Perform a few Hamstring Stretches every week to keep your legs and back limber.

Annotation Key
Bold text indicates target muscles
Black text indicates other working muscles
* indicates deep muscles

- Stand facing a Pilates chair with your feet in V-position. Place your hands on the pedals and inhale.
- Curl your back as you exhale and push down on the pedals.
- Hold for a few breaths and return to the starting position. Repeat 5 times.

gluteus maximus

gluteus medius*

erector spinae*

biceps femoris

gastrocnemius

soleus

444 Hamstring Stretch and Pulse
Stand facing a Pilates chair with your feet near the footrest. Place your hands on the pedals and inhale. Curl your back as you exhale and push down on the pedals. Pulse up and down for 10 counts: 5 counts on inhale, 5 on exhale.

445 Hamstring Stabilized Press
Stand facing a Pilates chair with your feet near the footrest. Place your hands on the pedals and lower your head so it touches the chair seat. Both elbows should be bent. Push the pedals down, maintaining your torso position. Pulse up and down 10 times.

446 Standing Hamstring Stretch
Place a box by a Pilates chair and step onto the box. Reach over the chair and push down on the pedals. Hold for a few breaths and return to the starting position. Repeat 5 times.

447 Cat on Chair
Kneel on a Pilates chair and reach your hands to the pedals. Inhale to prepare. Find your balance and exhale as you push down on the pedals. Return to the starting position and repeat 3 times.

448 Hamstring Pulls on Pedals
Lie with your feet on the pedals of a Pilates chair. Pull in your abs and press your back into the floor. Slowly push down on the pedals and return to the starting position. Repeat 10 times.

Long Stretch

You need substantial abdominal strength to maintain a long straight line from your head to your heels in this exercise. The Long Stretch also works your arms and shoulders as well as your glutes and hamstrings. This stretch calls for precision, concentration, and stamina.

Correct form
Pull your shoulder blades down your back. Try to isolate the movement in your shoulders.

Avoid
Don't lift your hips out of alignment with the rest of your body.

Annotation Key
Bold text indicates target muscles
Black text indicates other working muscles
* indicates deep muscles

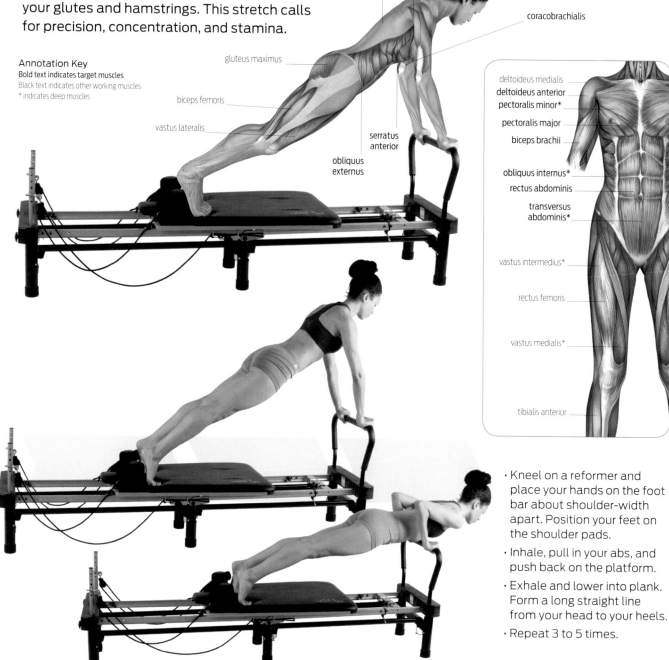

trapezius
triceps brachii
erector spinae*
coracobrachialis
gluteus maximus
biceps femoris
vastus lateralis
serratus anterior
obliquus externus

deltoideus medialis
deltoideus anterior
pectoralis minor*
pectoralis major
biceps brachii
obliquus internus*
rectus abdominis
transversus abdominis*
vastus intermedius*
rectus femoris
vastus medialis*
tibialis anterior

- Kneel on a reformer and place your hands on the foot bar about shoulder-width apart. Position your feet on the shoulder pads.
- Inhale, pull in your abs, and push back on the platform.
- Exhale and lower into plank. Form a long straight line from your head to your heels.
- Repeat 3 to 5 times.

450 Single-Leg Long Stretch

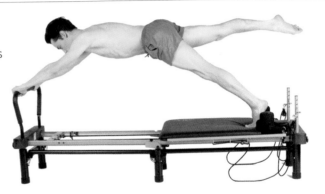

Kneel on a reformer and place your hands on the foot bar about shoulder-width apart. Rest your feet on the shoulder pads. Lift your right leg to hip height, inhale, and push back on the platform. Form a straight line from your head to your raised foot. Exhale on the return. Repeat 5 times.

451 Long Stretch Extensions

Kneel on a reformer and place your hands on the foot bar about shoulder-width apart. Rest your feet on the shoulder pads. Lift your left leg and right arm. Inhale as you push back on the platform. Exhale on the return. Alternate arms and legs, and repeat 5 times.

452 Long Back Stretch

Place your hands behind your back on the foot bar of a reformer. Position your feet on the shoulder pads. Inhale, scoop in your abs, and dip down as you push on the platform. Lift your hips to form a straight line from shoulders to ankles. Repeat 5 times.

453 Long Back Stretch with Leg Lifts

Place your hands behind your back on the foot bar of a reformer. Position your feet on the shoulder pads. Inhale, scoop in your abs, and dip down as you push on the platform. Lift your hips and raise your right leg. Return to the starting position and repeat 5 times.

454 Bull on Reformer

Stand on a reformer. Place your hands on the foot bar about shoulder-width apart. Put your left foot at the edge of the platform and right foot on a shoulder pad. Inhale as you push back on the platform. Exhale on the return. Alternate legs and repeat 5 times.

455 Elephant on Heels

Stand on a reformer. Place your hands on the foot bar, about shoulder-width apart, and press your feet flat into the shoulder pads. Inhale as you push back on the platform. Exhale on the return. Alternate legs and repeat 5 times.

456 Elephant on Tiptoes

Stand on a reformer. Place your hands on the foot bar, shoulder-width apart, and support your feet on tiptoe against the shoulder pads. Inhale as you push back on the platform. Exhale on the return. Alternate legs and repeat 5 times.

457 Elephant Arabesque

Stand on a reformer. Place your hands on the foot bar, shoulder-width apart, and support your feet against the shoulder pads. Inhale as you push back on the platform and lift your left leg. Exhale on the return and lower your leg. Repeat 5 times on each leg.

458 Frog Long Stretch

Stand on a reformer. Place your hands on the foot bar, shoulder-width apart. Press your heels together by the shoulder pads and turn out your toes. Inhale as you bend your knees outward and push back on the platform. Exhale on the return. Repeat 5 times.

459

Mermaid Twist

The Mermaid Twist on the reformer demands concentration and control as you balance on your side, twist your torso, and push on the platform at the same time. The Mermaid Twist is an excellent full-body workout, targeting the obliques in particular. Pull through your arms and legs, and feel the energy release from you body.

Annotation Key
Bold text indicates target muscles
Black text indicates other working muscles
* indicates deep muscles

obliquus internus*

tensor fasciae latae

tractus iliotibialis

pectineus*

sartorius

rectus femoris

vastus lateralis

deltoideus

transversus abdominis*

obliquus externus*

biceps brachii

brachioradialis

extensor digitorum

flexor digitorum

rectus abdominis

adductor longus

vastus medialis

brachialis

gracilis*

peroneus

gastrocnemius

soleus

- Sit on your right hip with ankles crossed and feet pressed against the headrest. Place your right hand on the foot bar.
- Inhale and lift your hips as you push out on the platform. Raise your left arm overhead.
- Exhale and twist your torso to your right, scooping your left arm under your torso.
- Repeat 3 times on each side.

460 Mermaid on Arc Barrel

Sit on the floor with an arc barrel on your right. Tuck your left foot behind your hip and cross your right leg in front of you. Raise your arms overhead. Slowly bend to your right from your waist and drape your side along the arc barrel. Articulate up and repeat 5 times on each side.

461 Mermaid Press and Stretch

Sit sideways on a reformer with your right shin pressed against the shoulder pads and your left leg crossed in front of you. Place your left hand on the foot bar. Push the platform away from the foot bar and reach your right arm overhead. Repeat 5 times on each side.

462 Mermaid Shoulder Press

Sit sideways on a reformer with your right shin pressed against the shoulder pads and left leg crossed in front of you. Place your hands on the foot bar. Push the platform away from the foot bar and return. Repeat 5 times on each side.

463 Mermaid Lift

Sit on your left hip with ankles crossed and feet against the shoulder pads. Place your left hand on the foot bar. Inhale and lift your hips as you push out on the platform. Raise your right arm overhead. Exhale and return to the starting position. Repeat 3 times per side.

464 Side Bend Seated
Sit sideways on a Pilates chair. Place your left hand on the pedal. As you exhale and push down, reach your right arm overhead. Return to the upright position and repeat 5 times on each side.

465 Side Bend with Chair
Kneel beside a Pilates chair. Press the pedal with your right hand and reach your left arm overhead. Return to the starting position and repeat 5 times on each side.

466 Seated Back Twist
Sit on a Pilates chair with legs forward and arms out to the sides. With your left hand, reach the pedal behind you and push down. Twist your torso to your left and reach your right arm overhead. Return to the seated position and repeat 5 times on each side.

467 Star Lift
Sit sideways on a reformer with ankles crossed and pressed against the shoulder pads. Place your left hand on the foot bar. Inhale and lift up as you push out on the platform. Extend your right arm and leg upward. Lower and repeat 3 times on each side.

468 Single-Arm Side Stretch
Sit on a reformer with your feet between the shoulder pads. Place your left hand on the foot bar behind you. Inhale and push the platform away, twisting your torso. Reach your right arm overhead. Return to the seated position and repeat 5 times on each side.

469

Barrel Squats

Flip your arc barrel upside-down for these challenging Barrel Squats. This exercise works your glutes and quads, as all squats do, but with the additional challenge of balancing on the arc barrel. These squats build pelvic stability as you focus on your powerhouse to stay balanced.

Annotation Key
Bold text indicates target muscles
Black text indicates other working muscles
* indicates deep muscles

Correct form
Lengthen your spine and pull your shoulder blades down. Push your weight into your heels.

Avoid
Try not to bring your knees in front of your feet as you squat down.

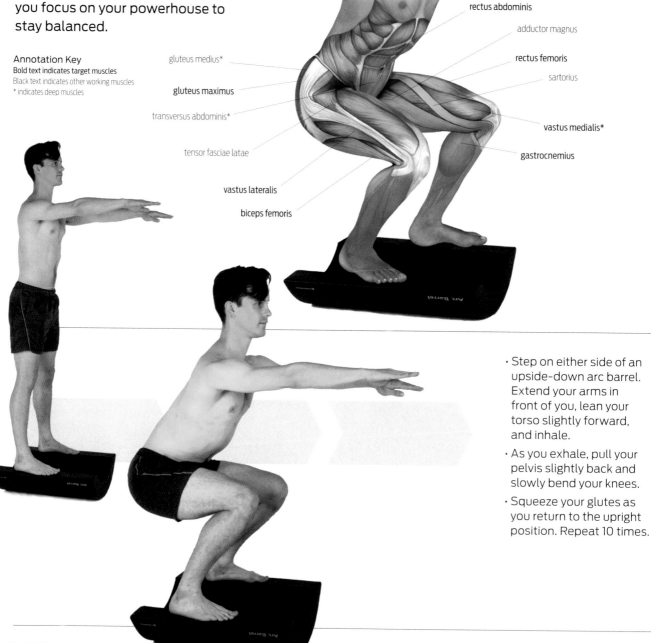

gluteus medius*

gluteus maximus

transversus abdominis*

tensor fasciae latae

vastus lateralis

biceps femoris

rectus abdominis

adductor magnus

rectus femoris

sartorius

vastus medialis*

gastrocnemius

- Step on either side of an upside-down arc barrel. Extend your arms in front of you, lean your torso slightly forward, and inhale.

- As you exhale, pull your pelvis slightly back and slowly bend your knees.

- Squeeze your glutes as you return to the upright position. Repeat 10 times.

470 Squatting Leg Press

The Squatting Leg Press demands precise movements and a lot of balance. The exercise increases the range of motion in your hip flexors and stretches out your hamstrings.

Mind-body connection

The vast majority of Pilates exercises demand full concentration. Mindful execution of the exercises benefits your form and increases your awareness of your body. Joseph Pilates believed that Contrology requires "the complete coordination of body, mind, and spirit," and that harmony leads to better overall health and well-being.

- Place your hands on top of a Pilates chair and your left foot on the pedal.
- Bend your right knee and balance your right foot on top of the chair.
- Press your left foot down on the pedal. Return to the starting position and repeat 5 times on each leg.

471 Squat Twist on Arc Barrel

Step on either side of an upside-down arc barrel. Place your arms at your sides. Lean your torso slightly forward and inhale. As you exhale, pull your pelvis slightly back, and slowly bend your knees. Twist your torso to the right and reach your hands to your right foot. Squeeze your glutes as you return to the upright position. Repeat 5 times to each side.

472 Tendon Stretch

Stand on the edge of a reformer platform and curl your torso forward. Reach your hands to the foot bar behind you. Push the platform forward as you lower your hips, shifting your weight from your feet to your hands. Return to the starting position and repeat 5 times.

473 Tendon Stretch Leg Lift

The Tendon Stretch Leg Lift works your glutes while stretching your hamstrings and Achilles tendons. Move slowly and deliberately to get the maximum benefit.

Joint mobility

One of the goals of Pilates is to increase joint mobility. Joints—the connections between bones—consist of muscles, ligaments, and cartilage. Every time you bend or turn, synovial fluid lubricates and nourishes your joints. A healthy range of motion prevents stiffness and protects against injury.

- Stand at the edge of a reformer platform and curl your torso forward. Place your hands on the foot bar behind you.
- Lift your left leg slightly and push the platform forward. As you lower your hips, shift your weight from your right foot to your hands.
- Return to the starting position and repeat 5 times on each leg.

474 Tendon Stretch on Chair

Stand on the pedals of a Pilates chair and place your hands on either side of the seat. Pull your hips up as you let the pedals rise upward. Push back down and repeat 10 times.

475 Tendon Stretch Leg Raise

Stand on the pedals of a Pilates chair and place your hands on either side of the seat. Extend your right leg to the side and lift your hips and as you let the pedal rise upward. Push back down and repeat 5 times on each leg.

476 Tendon Stretch Leg Extended

Step your right foot on a pedal of a Pilates chair and place your hands on either side of the seat. Extend your left leg behind you. Pull your hips up as you let the pedal rise. Push back down and repeat 10 times.

477

Chest Press on Reformer

The Chest Press on Reformer strengthens your chest and arm muscles. The Chest Press is a great introduction to more complex rowing exercises on the reformer.

Correct form
As you push out with your arms, engage your pecs. Pull your shoulder blades down.

Avoid
Don't contract your shoulder blades on the return.

iliopsoas*

pectineus*

sartorius

adductor longus

adductor brevis

gracilis*

vastus medialis

Annotation Key
Bold text indicates target muscles
Black text indicates other working muscles
* indicates deep muscles

deltoideus anterior

triceps brachii

pectoralis major

rectus abdominis

obliquus externus

obliquus internus*

transversus abdominis*

vastus intermedius*

rectus femoris

tensor fasciae latae

- Sit on the platform of a reformer with your lower back against the headrest.
- Put your hands in the straps and bend your elbows, with your hands close to your chest.
- Push through your shoulders and reach your arms forward at shoulder height.
- Return to the starting position and repeat 10 times.

Hug the Tree on Reformer

Sit on a reformer with your lower back against the shoulder pads. Hold the straps and extend your arms out to the sides at shoulder height, palms facing forward. Pull your arms forward and touch your fingertips in front of you, as if hugging a tree. Return to the starting position and repeat 10 times.

Shoulder Rotator on Reformer

Sit on a reformer with your lower back against the shoulder pads. Hold the straps. Press your elbows in at your sides and extend your forearms outward. Rotate your elbows, pulling your hands forward. Return to the starting position and repeat 10 times.

Basic Row on Reformer

Sit on a reformer with your feet on the headrest. Put your hands in the straps and extend your arms forward at waist height. Pull your arms back and bring your hands in toward your chest. Return to the starting position and repeat 10 times.

Shoulder Blade Shrug

Sit on a reformer and put your hands in the straps. Extend your arms forward at waist height. Shrug your shoulders up, keeping your arms extended forward. Shrug your shoulders up and down for 10 repetitions.

482 Reformer Rowing 1

Sit on a reformer with your lower back against the shoulder pads. Put your hands in the straps, bend your elbows, and raise your hands to your chest. In one smooth motion, push down through your shoulders, reach far forward, and circle your arms up. Return to the starting position and repeat 10 times.

483 Reformer Rowing 2

Sit on a reformer with your lower back against the shoulder pads. Put your hands in the straps, bend your elbows, and raise your hands to your chest. In one smooth motion, reach forward through your shoulders, lower your arms, and circle your arms up. Return to the starting position and repeat 10 times.

484 High-Elbow Row on Reformer

Sit on a reformer and hold the straps in front of you at shoulder height. Pull your arms back, keeping them at shoulder height. Return to the starting position and repeat 10 times.

485 Back Rowing 1

Back Rowing on the reformer feels very different from the strokes on a rowing machine. This exercise involves leaning far back while pulling on the straps, swinging arms out to the sides, and leaning forward. It's a vigorous workout for the whole body.

- Sit on a reformer and hold the straps at your chest, palms facing down.
- In one smooth motion, roll backward, keeping your hands at your chest, then open your arms wide; roll your torso forward and swing your arms in front of you.
- Return to the starting position and repeat 10 times.

486 Back Rowing 2

Sit on a reformer and hold the straps above eye level, palms facing your forehead. In one smooth motion, roll backward, keeping your hands near your face; roll forward as you extend your arms up, then swing your arms to the sides. Return to the starting position and repeat 10 times.

487 Single-Arm Back Rowing

Sit on a reformer and hold the straps at waist height. Twist your torso to the left and pull your left arm back toward your chest. Return to the starting position and repeat 10 times to each side.

488

Triceps Coordination

Triceps Coordination works a lot more than just the triceps. For much of this exercise, you will keep your head and legs raised, so your abs will get a serious workout too.

Correct form
Keep your head and neck off the platform during the repetitions. Press your heels together and point your toes outward.

Avoid
Don't strain your neck or hunch your shoulders.

Annotation Key
Bold text indicates target muscles
Black text indicates other working muscles
* indicates deep muscles

iliopsoas *
pectineus*
adductor magnus
adductor longus
sartorius
gracilis*
vastus medialis

vastus lateralis

transversus abdominis*

obliquus internus*

rectus abdominis

pectoralis major

rectus femoris

vastus intermedius*

tensor fasciae latae

obliquus externus

teres major

- Lie on a reformer with legs in tabletop position. Hold the straps and rest your elbows on the platform.
- Inhale and curl your head and neck up. Raise your legs to 45 degrees and push your arms forward.
- Open your legs and tap them together 3 times.
- Return your legs to tabletop and perform 5 repetitions.

Straight-Arm Lowers on Reformer

Lie on a reformer with legs in tabletop position. Hold the straps and extend your arms straight up. Pull your arms down to your sides, keeping your legs in tabletop. Return to the starting position and perform 10 repetitions.

490 T-Press

Lie on a reformer with legs in tabletop position. Hold the straps and extend your arms out to the sides. Pull your hands in toward your hips. Return to the starting position and perform 10 repetitions.

 ## T-Press Coordination

Lie on a reformer with legs in tabletop position. Hold the straps and open your arms and legs out to the sides. Curl your head and neck up as you pull your arms in toward your sides and press your legs together. Return to the starting position and perform 10 repetitions.

492 Reverse T-Raise

Lie on a reformer with legs in tabletop position. Hold the straps and extend your arms out to the sides. Draw your hands in toward your hips. Return to the starting position and perform 10 repetitions.

493 Arm Raise on Reformer

Lie on a reformer with legs in tabletop position. Hold the straps and rest your arms at your sides. Pull your arms up toward the ceiling. Return to the starting position and perform 10 repetitions.

494 Windmill Arm Raises

Lie on a reformer with legs in tabletop position. Hold the straps and rest your hands at your hips. Extend your arms out to the sides. Reach your right arm upward, then slowly lower back out to the side. Repeat with the left arm. Alternate arms, and perform 10 repetitions.

495 Triceps Kickback

Kneel on a reformer with your chest pressed into your thighs. Hold the straps near your thighs. Keeping your back straight, extend your arms behind you. Return to the starting position and repeat 10 times.

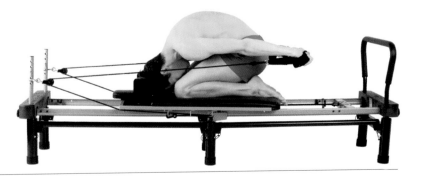

496

Chair Dips

Chair Dips tone your triceps, biceps, and chest muscles. In this exercise, you sit on the pedals of a Pilates chair to help push through the movement, so your glutes and quads get a workout too. Adjust the springs as necessary to achieve the desired resistance.

Correct form
Open your chest and tuck your elbows as you move down. Keep your chin up and gaze forward.

Avoid
Don't round your shoulders forward.

Annotation Key
Bold text indicates target muscles
Black text indicates other working muscles
* indicates deep muscles

deltoideus

triceps brachii

latissimus dorsi

rectus abdominis

obliquus externus

transversus abdominis*

pectoralis major

pectoralis minor*

coracobrachialis

deltoideus

biceps brachii

gluteus maximus

- Sit on the pedals of a Pilates chair and place your hands on the front edge of the seat.

- Inhale and push down on the pedals with your glutes while extending your right leg forward.

- Lift up and repeat with the opposite leg. Perform a total of 10 repetitions.

497 Dips on Pedals

Place your hands on the seat of a Pilates chair and rest your toes on the pedals. Press your heels together and turn out your toes in V-position. Inhale and push down on the pedals. Bend your knees out to the sides as you lower your body. Lift up and perform 10 repetitions.

498 Frog Dips

Sit on the edge of a Pilates chair and hold on to the hand supports. Place your feet on the pedals and turn out your toes in V-position. Inhale and push down on the pedals, keeping your torso stable. Lift up and perform 10 repetitions.

499 Triceps Press on Box

Sit on a box with your back to a Pilates chair and place your hands on the pedals behind you. Push down on the pedals. Return to the starting position and perform 10 repetitions.

500 Triceps Press with Split Pedal

Sit on a box with your back to a Pilates chair and place your hands on the pedals behind you. Push down on one pedal at a time, alternating hands. Perform 10 repetitions.

501 Long Back Stretch Dip

Sit on the edge of a reformer platform and place your hands behind you on the foot bar. Engage your abs, lift your torso, and push the platform away from you. Dip down for 5 repetitions and return to the starting position.

Index of Exercises

Credits

Photography

Naila Ruechel

Photography Assistant

Finn Moore

Models

Natasha Diamond-Walker
Abdiel Jacobson
Jessica Gambellur
Daniel Wright

Additional Photography

Page 7 Leah-Anne Thompson/Shutterstock.com
Page 10 zeljkodan/Shutterstock.com

Illustration

All anatomical illustrations by Hector Diaz/3DLabz Animation Limited
Full-body anatomy and Insets by Linda Bucklin/Shutterstock.com